THE CONSCIOUS STONE

THE
CONSCIOUS STONE

The Life of Edward William Godwin

by

DUDLEY HARBRON

He builded better than he knew;—
The conscious stone to beauty grew.
R. W. EMERSON

BENJAMIN BLOM, INC.
Publishers, New York 1971

First published London 1949
Reissued 1971 by
Benjamin Blom, Inc.
New York, N.Y. 10025

Library of Congress
Catalog Card Number 79-172551

Printed in the
United States of America

ACKNOWLEDGEMENTS

THIS LIFE of Edward William Godwin is based upon information collected over several years. The material from which to reconstruct the career of this remarkable man is widely scattered in place and time, but, happily enough, is recoverable.

That this has been possible is due to Godwin himself, for it was his habit to illustrate the theme upon which he wrote or spoke by incidents from his own experience. At the time of delivery these reminiscences added point: to-day they provide particulars, otherwise unrecorded, relating to his childhood, boyhood, and early manhood. For the facilities to examine these confessions I have to thank Mr. E. J. Carter, B.A., and the Staff of the Library of the Royal Institute of British Architects, who have posted me large numbers of the building publications in which they were printed, and Mr. James Ross, M.A., who has sent me the scarce printed works of Godwin, and searched the Directories and files of the Bristol newspapers for any reference.

Over the succeeding period—his years of partnership with Henry Crisp, 1864–71, and for a year earlier and several years later, there is extant the whole of the correspondence of the firm. To all of these thousands of letters I have had access, thanks to the kind offices of Sir George Oatley, LL.D., F.R.I.B.A., their owner.

Most of the letters were written by Crisp, a few by Godwin ; some from dictation by either partner ; and together they provide a complete record of Godwin's professional life over the years covered by the correspondence. In addition there is a considerable body of orally transmitted anecdotage dealing with the same period.

With Sir George Oatley I have visited the scenes of Godwin's life in Bristol, and have been told by him in conversation and correspondence all that is remembered of Godwin and his associates in Bristol. Sir George Oatley has generously placed at my disposal such of Edward Godwin's drawings as remain in his keeping. For all his invaluable help I would thank him. Other unpublished facts are due to the extracts from the Minutes of the Bristol Society of Architects, made by Mr. A. J. Knott, F.R.I.B.A.

For the Herefordshire interval Ellen Terry's *Memoirs* and Mr. Graham Robertson's *Time Was* must be consulted, since they deal with matters, which transpired before, during and after the term of the letters of the firm, from a different point of view. The first draft of the manuscript of this book was read by the late Miss Edith Craig, who graciously gave me some notes and corrections which have been incorporated in its pages. Some reminiscences of the same period have been communicated by Sir Edwin Pascoe and Mr. F. Stobart, A.R.I.B.A.

The rest of his life is traceable in the publications of the time to which he contributed, or in which he was reported. In his letters, and his comings, and goings, and sayings as recorded. In addition there are fragmentary references to him in the works of his contemporaries. Oscar Wilde, the Pennell's *Whistler Journal*, Louise Jopling's *Twenty Years of My Life*, and several other memoirs acknowledged in the text.

More than one portrait of him was drawn from life by Raffles Davison, and one of these his daughter, Mrs. Nora Horn, has kindly allowed me to reproduce.

A few of his buildings can be seen; others that have been destroyed or altered, or never built, may be studied in the illustrations of their plans, sections and elevations, and in several instances from the original drawings.

A like opportunity is afforded by the furniture he designed, illustrations of which survive, and actual specimens have been photographed through the kindness of Mrs. Lewis Clarke, who has told me something of their associations. Unfortunately, I have been unable to trace the whereabouts of other pieces of his furniture, despite enquiry by letter and advertisement.

Of his designs for wallpaper a number are preserved as illustrations; until recent times there were actual specimens, the present whereabouts of which are unknown. To the generosity of Mr. A. V. Sugden and Mr. E. A. Entwhistle, is due the illustration of the wallpaper design contained in the former's valuable *History of English Wallpaper*.

With rare exceptions Godwin's interior decorations remain solely in verbal descriptions and inadequate illustrations. His contributions to the other arts appear to survive only in illustrations of costume, stage setting, designs for various household requisites—or adjuncts of architecture. It is to be hoped that, if any of these have escaped destruction, they will be preserved.

All these relics, together with the official papers relating to birth, marriage and death, deeds and documents have been considered in order to give as complete a picture as is possible of the man and his work.

Owing to the kind permission of the Hon. Mrs. Hervey-Bathurst, I am able to reproduce the picture of Kate and Ellen Terry—*The Sisters* by G. F. Watts, R.A.

Help of various kinds has been given by many friends who have answered my enquiries or volunteered information within their knowledge. The Rev. K. L. Parry, Mrs. Alice Ionides, Mr. Basil Ionides, F.R.I.B.A., Mr. James Laver, Mr. L. E. Berman, Miss Christopher St. John, Mr. John Summerson, F.S.A., Professor Henry-Russell Hitchcock, Mr. F. H. Allen F.R.I.B.A., Mr. W. A. Pite, F.R.I.B.A., Mr. R. R. Meadows, A.R.I.B.A., Mr. Cyril Farthing, Mr. G. D. Ruding Bryan, Miss E. M. Holmes, Mr. H. D. Priestman, A.R.I.B.A., and Mr. A. K. Bray.

To all of them I would express my thanks for the interest they have shown and the aid they have given so freely.

G. DUDLEY HARBRON.

CONTENTS AND ILLUSTRATIONS

The late
E·W·Godwin

" IF A MAN is master of his profession, he cannot be ignorant that he is so; and, if he is not employed by those who pretend to encourage art, he will employ himself, and laugh in secret at the pretences of the ignorant, while he has every night dropped in his shoe, as soon as he puts it off, and puts out the candle, and gets into bed, a reward for the labours of the day such as the world cannot give, and patience and time await to give him all the world can give."

WILLIAM BLAKE

INTRODUCTION

THE CENTRAL figure in this book, Edward William Godwin, died in 1886, yet although near sixty years have passed since his death, no biography of him has appeared. The omission is odd, for his life was eventful, his attainments remarkable and his personality colourful.

His name must be known to any who have read the essays of Sir Max Beerbohm, or the works of Oscar Wilde, that contain his collected papers under their embracing titles, *Art and Decoration*, *Intentions* and *Reviews*.

Wilde, who knew Godwin well, refers to him as " one of the most artistic spirits of this century in England " (*Intentions*, The Truth of Masks, p. 238), and, as such, constantly calls upon his work to support his own arguments; and even more emphatically, Sir Max Beerbohm, in his essay *1880*, draws attention to him as " Godwin that superb architect . . . the greatest aesthete of them all ".

Yet when the reader's curiosity has been aroused by these pregnant statements, and he seeks to supplement them or dispel his ignorance by turning to the *Dictionary of National Biography*, he finds only a meagre account of the architect's career, which leaves him puzzled as to why it was written, and fails entirely to explain the enthusiasm of such connoisseurs as Wilde and Beerbohm.

Reasons may be surmised for the omission of his longer-lived contemporaries to put on record their recollections of so notable a figure. They may have thought his artistic powers to be so widely recognised as to need no telling, or some friend better qualified to be employed on the task, or merely that it was none of their business. Possibly they agreed that the day was not favourable.

At the time of his death, which was premature, there were those left behind who, it was felt, might be injured or offended should his story be told ; moreover, the mood of the time was hypocritical. The critics were unable to dissociate conduct and capacity. Further, about the date of his death, the aesthetic movement, with which his name had grown to be associated, was under a cloud, the more dense because it was artificially accentuated by commercial interests apprehensive for their future. These interests feared that the aesthetic movement would injure their trade in fabrics, furniture, fashion and the arts of the stage. They did not want so disturbing an epoch to be remembered—save in derision.

The passing of time did not increase the regard or clear away the misconceptions. Rather, the numbers of the censorious public grew when Wilde, who had assumed the cloak of a prophet of the cult of beauty, was sentenced to imprisonment. The respectable citizen concluded that the aesthetic movement had been a dangerous conspiracy. When, some years after the Wilde trial, Walter Pater died, *The Times* (31st July 1894) reminded the nation of his part in the movement. " That his influence was always healthful, we do not pretend to say." Even so recently as 1906 Pater's biographer, A. C. Benson, did not dare discuss " actions by the canons of what was held to be beautiful " ; although he did forecast that the time would come " when we can look dispassionately at the part which the aesthetic school had played in the mental development of the age ".

All this nervous hostility succeeded in burying the name of Godwin, " the greatest aesthete of them all ", along with a vague legend of long-haired poets, ineffectual artists and languorous Mayfair poseurs, the type described by the humourless Holman Hunt as " talking in mincing affectation and adopting a tone which they stamped as that of extreme ' culture ' ; these busy jackanapes were characterised in a spirit of irony as ' unutterably utter ' " (*The Pre-Raphaelite Brotherhood*, Holman Hunt, p. 364). So widespread was this type of criticism of the aesthetes that even now many people believe that Hunt and those who thought like him had said all that there was to say about them.

This oblivion would be of little consequence if the accusations were true, but since it results from a distortion of the facts it becomes serious in the light of history. The follies of some of the hangers-on may have provided the excuse to damn them, but the movement was not damned, save in the minds of those incapable of distinguishing truth from falsehood; these last are sufficiently numerous to have encouraged a misreading of artistic development through the omission to deal with a most important phase of art or to understand the ideas and works of those who were its active exponents.

There are indications that these misconceptions are dispersing. Wilde's claim that life imitates art, and not art life, is increasingly admitted to be a profound truth, and not, as the Philistine would have us believe, an absurd statement. Roger Fry concluded " that under certain conditions the rhythm of life and art may coincide with great effect on both; but in the main the two rhythms are distinct, and as often as not play against each other ". More recently Mr. Ernest Newman has said—" The fallacy that art takes its clue from life, and that as the latter is the former will consequently be, was disposed of long ago by Oscar Wilde." It is for the artist the only self-respecting philosophy. The realisation of its consequence is the eternal insignia of art.

Living, as he did, during an interval of time that in the history of art is deemed to have been deplorable, Edward Godwin is an instance of the truth of the contention of his friend Whistler, that there are only artists and not artistic periods. This was in turn an aspect of Wilde's conviction. The inner urge of the artist to express his intuitions is irresistible, and it is hardly affected by external appearances. Those persons who are influenced are not the creators but the receptive spectators. Art is the element in the work that exists for its own sake and not for any utilitarian purpose. It is the energy that endlessly provokes in the percipient the ideas which " motivated the artist ".

Because Edward Godwin realised these axioms he was able to appraise the quality in the creations of cultures widely separated in time and place. He was one of the first designers to recognise that the machine is a tool, and that its employment to simulate manual work injures both the new and the old, in which attitude he differed from William Morris. It is true that in his profuse writings Godwin does not place any undue emphasis upon the structural basis of design. He had been trained early by an engineer, and because this had been his upbringing, the need to enlarge upon structure was not evident. He stressed instead the effect of form and colour upon the mind as apprehended through the eye, and his outstanding gift was the ability to awaken interest through form, which faculty he employed in the arrangement of material in building, of objects in an apartment, or of individuals upon a stage. His fellows could apprehend, when it was expressed, a message they could not voice themselves.

Architectural appreciation is nearly as rare as architecture. It is handicapped since the cost of its realisation bears no relation to the income of its appreciators. Those who enjoy may be such as cannot afford, while those who can afford may lack selective courage. In part from this, and in part from temperament, Godwin lacked architectural opportunity, although he made the most of every opportunity he had. He was an architect's architect. A greater use of his services would have speeded the renaissance of architecture. As it was, lack of patronage encouraged him to turn his talent toward furniture, wallpaper, costume and stage design.

The appeal of colour and form presented in movement or living picture is less abstract than in architecture, and although the spectacle is fugitive, it can be seen repeatedly by a large number of spectators whose object is to see and hear. Concentrated attention is especially necessary in the case of plays performed in the open air. Godwin in using these vehicles to advance his aesthetic object was the first architect since Inigo Jones to employ the stage. Pugin had used stage setting merely to support the Gothic revival, but Godwin, as will appear, had a wider intention.

The objects of Pugin, Ruskin, Morris and Godwin were the same—namely to elevate the taste of their generation. In many respects the means they used were akin. Pugin, Morris and Godwin wrote, spoke, designed and trained craftsmen to execute their designs. All three made with their own hands some of the things they had designed. They differed in that Pugin employed a mystic religious approach interspersed by appeals to the nation to return to the days of the maypole. Ruskin eloquently moved the self-improving middle classes and scolded or patronised the artisan; Morris spent his strength in encouraging the operative to employ his hands in making things of use and beauty. All three sought their inspiration in the past.

Godwin's efforts were directed to the conversion of the young people of his profession, and to the cultivated members of lay society. He addressed himself to that small section which, preserving a remnant of the perception of the eighteenth century, had set an example.

The public, he believed, had been corrupted by the Press in its appeal to the unthinking, its praise of the mediocre, and its disparagement of the able.

Opening with a dispute as to the merit of the Elgin Marbles, Greece or Rome, the conflict drifted into one between classic and Gothic—the Battle of the Styles—followed in mid-century by the Crystal Palace which set at issue the architect and the engineer. Ultimately the attack was directed against the designer of the White House, the nocturne by its owner, and the claim of the aesthetes to selective discrimination.

What is common to all these protests is that the thing attacked is new and differs from that formerly accepted. Discussing the possible reason for the similar reaction from the post-impressionists, Roger Fry observed " People felt that their special culture was one of their social assets ", and when the foundations were disturbed they reacted uneasily. This is the equivalent on the intellectual plane to the hostility at the material level.

The span of Edward Godwin's life extended over all these phases. Moreover his creative activity was employed in most of the arts. The singular omission of his name or reference to his contributions from the pages of the histories of nineteenth-century art renders them suspect as partial or inadequate. That they are consciously partial at this date is unlikely—their partiality is a legacy from the past, the outcome of the persistent log-rolling of other reputations. That they are inadequate is not to be denied. Any reader sufficiently curious to turn to the building and architectural periodicals of his time cannot fail to remark the ubiquity of his name and works, or the unique quality of his designs. The most prolonged search will not produce his equal among his contemporaries, even those familiar favoured of his time, Scott, Street, or Burges. The superior virtues of his mind and his infinitely more extensive activity are manifest beyond question.

Even yet, forgotten, neglected or ignored, his legacy benefits his successors ; it is time that they should realise the part he played in " the mental development of the age ".

CHAPTER I

EARLY DAYS

IN A gas-lit room in Manchester, on a November evening in the year 1878, a crowded gathering of architects and students awaited with curiosity the entrance of the distinguished visitor who had been invited to talk to them. They were all agog to see for themselves what he looked like, and to hear what he had to say. For although in the flesh he was to many of them a stranger, to all of them his was a familiar name, Edward William Godwin. Besides, while few had met him, everyone had heard of his accomplishments, seen the evidence of his works and read some of his opinions. He was, indeed, a public figure and, as such, the subject of discussion among his fellows, who, as was their habit, either admired him intensely or thought his views outrageous. The critics were divided generally into the factions of youth and age.

At length, accompanied by the officials of the Architectural Association, he entered—a tall, slender, handsome, bearded man, past middle age. " Elegant " best described their impression of the man.

After his formal introduction to the audience by the chairman, their guest rose and began to speak—" Our surroundings in childhood have much to do with art ".[1]

The opening surprised. Then the gas jets waned, the candles took their place and the assembly was transported by the speaker into the past—the early years of Victoria's reign.

.   .   .   .   .   .

Undoubtedly when we are at an age curious to relate external objects to each other and ourselves, environment is the

[1] *The British Architect*, November 29th, 1878, p. 210.

text-book from which we begin to learn about our world, and the lessons then learned persist in our subconscious for the rest of life. So it had been with Edward Godwin.

His own childhood had begun in the reign of William IV, in the heart of the old city of Bristol where he was born on 26th May 1833, at 12 Old Market Street. It was a small unpretentious Georgian house, the face of which was flush with the pavement flanking the street. He was a delicate child. Within a month of his birth, on 20th June, he was carried by his parents, William and Ann Jones Godwin, to the nearby perpendicular Parish Church, St. Philip and St. Jacob, and then baptised at the old Norman font by the Vicar, the Reverend S. E. Day. The names chosen for him were Edward William, but it was by the first of these names that he was afterwards known in his family— obviously to avoid confusion with that of his father, William.

At the time of his son's birth, William Godwin was engaged in business as a currier and leather cutter. The Directories and Poll Books of the day confirm this description of his occupation, although the entry in the register of the Church of St. Philip describes him simply as a currier. He appears to have succeeded his father, John Godwin, in the undertaking which had been established in Bristol by that worthy in the latter years of the eighteenth century. Thus Edward's father and grandfather were both dealers in leather.

As if this were not a suitable ancestry for an artist, it has been claimed that William Godwin was by profession a decorator. The claim may have some substance, for there was in Bristol at 71 Old Market Street, before and after 1833, a firm styled Godwin, Smith and Co., Tilers, Plasterers and Painters, and William Godwin probably had some financial interest in the business that accounts for the name Godwin in the partnership, and has given rise to the legend; in any event, Edward, later in life, described his father as a builder.

Still William Godwin's association with the firm was brief and slender, for when Edward was but a child, his father retired from business to cultivate his garden.

The leather trade was flourishing, " more tanned leather was sold in the Leather Hall the first Tuesday in March and September than at any other place in the Kingdom ". So, like the shrewd man he was, Mr. Godwin gave up trading at the peak of his prosperity, and went to live at Earl's Mead House, a residence situated on the north-eastern outskirts of the city, with a large garden that ran down to the bank of the River Frome. It was here that Edward grew to boyhood.

His earliest recollections were of this garden. The land surrounding Earl's Mead, which took its name from its ancient designation, was decorated by relics—" fragments and crumbling bits from old churches " that William Godwin had thought proper to collect and preserve by arranging about his grounds. Doubtless these oddments were the perquisites of the partner in the firm of builders, for, as a seafaring man when he establishes himself on shore, erects a flagpole, and decorates his garden with an anchor ; so he, whether he had been a currier turned decorator or no, employed his leisure as an incipient antiquarian and collector. Indeed he was so careful for the preservation of his garden and the ruins he had saved, that he would not allow his children, two boys and a girl, to play in it unattended. Naturally they grew to look upon admission to that sanctuary as a special event. For Edward the unconscious stones came to have a mysterious attraction as an element of his " surroundings in childhood " ; they formed the setting for his imaginative games. Memories of the garden at Earl's Mead persisted with him until the end of his life. At the present date the whole area has become industrialised, the garden is built over—and only a fragment of the house, much altered, remains of Earl's Mead.

The boy had been born at an eventful period in history, when the externals of life were changing rapidly, and the social structure of the eighteenth century, constructed on an agricultural found-ation, was disintegrating. The introduction of machinery into industries previously dependent upon hand labour had greatly increased the volume of commodities available. Their manu-facture had drawn from the country to the towns the more enterprising of the population. Bristol alone had added 20,000 inhabitants in the last ten years, and the place had grown over-crowded. No one knew what steps to take to deal with the

dilemma, for none could foresee the ultimate towards which the
new inventions were thrusting the nation.

The City was in a disturbed state. Eighteen months before
Edward's birth, Bristol had been the scene of riot and bloodshed,
her Member of Parliament having stupidly implied that his
constituents were not wishful for Reform. This was more
than the less fortunate citizens could stomach and in order to make
their views quite plain, the mob had burned down the Mansion
House, the Bridewell and the City Gaol, and would have, if they
could, burned down the Bishop's Palace and the Cathedral on
College Green. But the more peaceable citizens had resisted. A
hundred heads were broken, several lives were lost, and more
buildings were damaged before the disturbance was quelled.
William Godwin often told the tale of these exciting times to his
children. Edward later could confirm his memory of these
fireside talks as he read the account of their occurrence put
down by Charles Kingsley, who had been a schoolboy at
Clifton when they happened—" the flame increased, multiplied
—at one point after another; till by ten o'clock that night I
seemed to be looking down upon Dante's Inferno, and to hear
the multitudinous moan and wail of lost spirits surging to and
fro amid the sea of fire ".

It had been a dangerous uprising, for old Bristol was closely
built, narrow streets and alleys crowded down to the quay on
the River Frome, the waterway that had made the place the
second city in England during the reign of Queen Elizabeth.

Fortunately the area of the fires had been controlled, so that
in Edward's childhood the old-world character of the city had
barely been disturbed—" it was not difficult to trace every line
of wall, each street and lane, the places of the towers, the churches,
the convents, the halls, the gates, the conduits, and the public
latrines. Old and decayed as was the Temple Street approach
from the railway, it was entirely more pleasant to the eye ",[1]
are his own words written in recollection of his native place.
They omit, however, an aspect of the city noticeable to an out-
sider, its hilly character. William Cobbett had observed this—
" it surpasses all that I ever saw. A great commercial city in the

midst of cornfields, meadows and woods, and the ships coming into the centre of it, miles away from anything like sea, up a narrow river, and passing between two clefts of rock probably a hundred feet high, so that from the top of these clefts you look down upon the main-topgallant masts of lofty ships that are gliding along ".

The City was not entirely mediaeval or Elizabethan in character in the early days of Victoria. It only seems so because those distant days, during Edward's boyhood, were claiming increased attention from people who felt that romance was being lost. In reality Bristol was graced by several squares of fine Georgian houses; Queen's Square in the centre, with an equestrian statue of William III; Brunswick and Portland Squares on the east, the latter only recently flanked by a neo-Gothic church of very interesting design; Berkeley Square to the west, bordered by stately houses whose stepped, rusticated ground floor faced the central tree-studded green. Then there were separate single buildings—the Corn Exchange which had been designed by John Wood of Bath; the Theatre Royal constructed by a nameless builder, and the simple room built on trust by John Wesley. Now, however, these renaissance works were disregarded by critics who considered themselves to be the arbiters of taste; they were felt to lack imagination.

Just as the eighteenth-century men had grown oblivious of the brilliance of the Middle Ages, so the early nineteenth had become indifferent to the work of their immediate predecessors. They thought it to be monotonous when they thought about it at all, and had discovered merit in the long-neglected Gothic. The unfortunate Bristol poet, Chatterton, was now their hero; and Blaize Hamlet, which John Nash had designed for Mr. Harford as a model of an old-world village round a green, four miles away to the north, was recommended as a spectacle all should see and admire. Its architect, Nash, was credibly reported to have said no palace he had ever planned had imparted to him a pleasure comparable to that which he derived from this humble employment of his talents and ingenuity. When he unburdened himself of this sentiment he was probably mindful of his unhappy experience over Buckingham House.

The unpleasant fact was that the picturesque Middle Ages and the ordered Augustan days were both of the past. A different set of values was ruthlessly gaining the ascendancy and the days of tall ship and mail coach were numbered. Before Edward was five years old the first steamship voyaged from Bristol to America, and by the time he was eight, London and Bristol were joined by a railway. Both these undertakings were designed by the same man, the engineer, I. K. Brunel. Like the rest of his countrymen, William Godwin was much impressed by these remarkable innovations, so completely so, that he resolved that Edward, when he grew old enough, should be trained to follow in the great man's profession.

" Engineering," he declared, " is more paying than architecture." In holding this opinion he was not singular. *The Bristol Guide* of his time says candidly, " Industry has, from the earliest period, distinguished the inhabitants of Bristol, and has formed their character at the same time that it has increased their wealth. Wherever a thirst for accumulation predominates, it engenders a sort of disdain for whatever is not immediately profitable ; and the study of letters and respect for the fine arts are consequently maintained only by the few." He was a practical man. He probably began to repent of the stones he had sentimentally put in his garden and was nervously apprehensive lest his son should choose to follow architecture as a career.

The boy already showed signs of artistic inclination, spending most of his time scribbling on any piece of paper he could find. Friends said that he had uncanny ability. When he wanted a subject to copy he found it in the pages of *Knight's Monthly Volume for all Readers*, to which the family subscribed. The number which pleased him most was devoted to the *History of British Costume from the Earliest Period to the Close of the Eighteenth Century*, by J. R. Planché, Esq., F.S.A.

He was enthralled by the pictures of men and women in strange dress and spent hours drawing them, colouring his drawings and cutting them out to make little figures with which to play. Unconsciously, while amusing himself, he was learning to draw and storing in his mind the images of what men and women had worn in past times. Two of the paper-backed copies of this shilling monthly were his first books.

When his father was called upon to admire these juvenile productions he consoled himself by the reflection that these childish preferences would soon pass. A few years at school and the boy would be drawing engines, bridges, ships, and other more manly objects. Every child who dresses up does not emerge as an actor.

So, when the day came for him to go to Exton School at Highbury, the instructions given to the headmaster were to prepare his pupil for a life devoted to engineering. Maybe he would emulate the feats of the great Brunel.

To all outward appearances Edward was quite ready to follow the path his father wanted him to travel. If Euclid were the guide-book to the road, then he carried his books about with him in his pocket. William Godwin's fears were abated.

Like most boys Edward was a romantic. His head was full of fancies of Earl's Mead as it had been, Chatterton and his discoveries, and the Elizabethan adventurers who had set out from Bristol. It was all so much more picturesque than the present reality. He had more curiosity than is usual in childhood for detailed information about the past. What, for instance, were those queer bits of stone in the garden at home ? If it was known what kinds of clothes men had worn, it must be equally possible to learn something about their buildings. He could see what they had been like any day of the week, for Bristol was a museum of architecture. As if in answer to his quest he came upon a small illustrated handbook, Bloxham's *Principles of Gothic Architecture*, which seemed likely to give him some clues. It had belonged to his father, and contained pictures of fragments of stone carving similar to those " cusps " and " crockets " ornamenting the garden, indicating how these had formed parts of the larger features of the building, the windows and the pinnacles. It mentioned Bristol Cathedral which he could visit. Moreover the book gave him a secret knowledge that other boys had not got.

By what seemed a fortunate chance, across the road from school there was a chapel in course of construction. Through the window of the classroom, Edward watched the men at work, and listened dreamily to the tinkle of their trowels. Day after day he saw the chapel rise from the foundations to the roof, and before his eyes the chaos grew to a recognisable whole. It was fascinating to see how the stone and brick, timber and plaster were transformed into the shape of a building, but he had no idea how this miracle was performed ; [indeed, at the time he had no notion that the building had an author. It was in fact a neo-Gothic structure, Highbury Chapel, the foundation stone of which had been laid on 3rd October 1842, the first to be realised by a young architect called William Butterfield (1814–1900). It is a simple stone building perpendicular in character, unlike its designer's later work.

When his schooldays were over, as a preliminary step on the road mapped out by his father, Edward was articled to William Armstrong, City Surveyor, Architect and Civil Engineer. The office was situated at 7 Brunswick Square—adjoining Pembroke Street—not more than half a mile from Edward's home, from which he walked daily. Although he claimed to be surveyor, architect and general indispensable, Mr. Armstrong was, above all, an able engineer. He was an elderly man, or so he appeared to his young pupil, and his special recommendation for Godwin senior was that he was a friend of the great Brunel who had built the railway to Bristol, flung the bridge over the Avon, and designed the steamship which had gone out from the port to America—an extraordinary series of accomplishments. In selecting Mr. Armstrong as a preceptor for his boy, he was convinced that a more fortunate choice could not have been made, for although his advertisement claimed proficiency as an architect, that gentle-man knew nothing at all about the art as then professionally understood. He was versed neither in the mysteries of classic orders, nor in the intricacies of Gothic vaulting. " He was a practical man, his walls were alright and his construction was generally good."[1]

But Armstrong's lack of architectural scholarship, or his friendship with Brunel, did not operate in the way that Edward's father had expected. There was architectural work to be done if the firm's claim to the title were to be respected.

[1] *The British Architect*, November 29th, 1878, p. 210.

Since Mr. Armstrong could not, or would not, design buildings himself, nor did any of the assistants or other pupils show a talent for architecture, he decided to leave that side of the business in the hands of the new young man who had read Bloxham. Naturally Edward felt flattered.

He had learned at home and at school the elements of geometric drawing, and it only needed practice to turn him into a draughtsman. He was already able to use all the instruments, tee squares, set squares, and compasses, and he understood how to draw a plan, section and elevation to scale. Thus, almost from the first, he was engaged in making William Armstrong's good constructional ideas presentable, and soon after in making his own ideas constructional. He was fertile in invention, or what passed off as invention, though in reality it was but recollection of things seen.

But imagination was not enough. Self-confident though he was, he soon discovered that he needed to know much more about building than had come within his range. These creations of his had to be constructed to enclose space, stand up, and resist the elements, before they could be of any use. As the other members of the staff could not give him much help he was left to his own devices.

Fortunately he was capable of self-criticism, which faculty, the basis of considered design, he never lost. He realised that the most speedy way to fill the gaps in his knowledge must be by recourse to books. The first two he read were Nicholson's *Five Orders* and *Carpentry*. Over them he pored nightly. Then, in order to get some knowledge of the procedure of professional practice, he studied Wightwick's *Hints to Young Architects* and the same writer's *The Palace of Architecture*, for Armstrong put the management of the office architectural work in his pupil's inexperienced charge. It was no doubt encouraging to Edward's vanity to discover himself so trusted, though to enable him to fulfil his employers' expectations he had to burn the midnight oil. These premature responsibilities were not his only care, for since an understanding of Gothic forms was becoming more necessary, even in such a practice as that of Armstrong—who had made some extraordinary alterations to St. Philip's Church,

substituting one arch for two—Edward re-read Bloxham's little
book and extended his study to Parker's *Glossary*, neither of
which contained the information he needed.

For it was on the practical side that he found himself least
informed ; indeed, how could it have been otherwise when he
had had no experience ? Problems were frequently cropping
up, the solutions to which he could not find in books. Op-
portunely someone told him to measure existing work in order to
study the means adopted, and solutions found, by others under
difficulties similar to his own. It was design in reverse, this
measuring of actual building ; drawing out you could see by what
means the effect had been secured, and if required, from the
drawing, be repeated. Thus prompted he measured some of
the antiques in Bristol, and on his half-days and during his holidays
he commenced to visit the neighbourhood on foot. Walking was
the only way he could travel (using Clevedon as a centre) to
Weston, Clapton, Portbury, Yatton and Nailsea in each of which
places he could collect information. He enjoyed the work
because it took him to fresh places in the open air, gave him an
objective, and resulted in a useful addition to his knowledge,
because when he reached his destination, he spent the day
sketching, measuring and plotting out on the site any buildings
that appealed to him, or answering the questions posed by the
work to be done in the office in Brunswick Square.

In this way he analysed the construction of roof and porches,
observed the jointing of stonework, and made notes of such items
as he hoped would be of use in the future. By re-using the means
that had stood the test of wind and weather, wear and tear, for
years, he could not go far wrong.

His persistent engagement in measuring was noticed by people
older than himself, and, though only yet a boy, he was asked by
one of them to help to illustrate a book. This was an ambitious
venture. *The Architectural Antiquities of Bristol and Neighbourhood*, a work which was published by subscription in 1851. The
book was dedicated by the authors, W. C. Burder, James Hine
and E. W. Godwin to the Duke of Beaufort.

The contributors optimistically promised to extend the work
by a further five parts, making six in all. Notwithstanding that

the first part was well supported by over two hundred subscribers, some of whom bought more than one copy, the remaining five promised parts never appeared. Why, is not known. The publication consisted of some few pages of letterpress commenting upon the theme of each of the six plates which illustrated the book. The material for two of the plates was contributed by each of the artists. Mr. Burder engraved the whole of the plates, and may also have edited the letterpress. Edward's share in the enterprise consisted of drawings to scale of the doorway, north porch, of St. Mary, Redcliffe, over which the manuscript on which Chatterton had exercised his imagination was reputed to have been found by the poet's father. One drawing showed the porch, and the other illustrated in more detail three carved capitals from the same porch. If the reproductions fairly represent the originals, these last must have been distinctly creditable. In all likelihood they were, for the engraver Burder was a perspective artist, an etcher, who perforce reproduced what he was shown by Edward's scale drawings.

That this undertaking should be deemed worthwhile indicated the growth of interest in the work of mediaeval builders, and the change of outlook over the years since Edward's birth.

William Armstrong was properly impressed by this evidence of his pupil's ability and expressed his approval by subscribing for an Imperial quarto proof copy. Mrs. Godwin bought one on India paper, and some other relatives subscribed.

William Godwin was reconciled by now to his younger boy's choice of architecture and had transferred his hopes to his elder son—who was fulfilling his father's programme. Mr. Godwin had early sensed Edward's preference and tried to divert it when he used the most powerful argument in the armoury of a commercial man, the financial, and had exclaimed, " Engineering is more paying than Architecture ". The appeal had been lost on Edward who was little interested in making money. He was, however, enthusiastic about art and architecture. Engineering as his profession was already for him a memory of the past, for he had by accident found an occupation congenial to his nature.

Owing to the peculiar circumstances obtaining in Mr. Armstrong's office, and the absence of any teaching facilities in

Bristol, Edward had to rely entirely upon his own efforts. He extended his reading, and studied the work of Rickman the insurance clerk who had classified the phases of Gothic architecture, of Barr on *Church Furniture*, and some serial publications one of which was *The Churches of the Archdeaconry of Northampton*. To most people they seemed dull reading, but for Edward they were revealing and fascinating.

By 1851 the Gothic revival had already become the main interest of many architects and was in process of attracting the rest. Its advocates had been very persistent and had fostered a fashion of pseudo-mediaeval art in those circles in which thirty years earlier Gothic had been, even in its genuine remains, regarded as illiterate. They had almost succeeded in making it fashionable to tour England, and to measure English work as had been Edward's mode of training, instead of going on the Grand Tour.

The man who had brought about this condition of architectural opinion, Augustus Welby Pugin, had just died at the age of forty. His last manifesto had been the arrangement of the mediaeval court at the Crystal Palace, his Magnum Opus the decorations and furnishing of the Palace of Westminster.

When Edward had been in his cradle, Welby Pugin had been meditating the deplorable taste of his countrymen from his home, St. Marie's Grange, Salisbury. It was from this personally designed Gothic grange, surrounded by monk's benches, refectory tables and pseudo-mediaeval hangings, that he had commenced his crusade.

Then and there he wrote and illustrated *Contrasts*, an architectural plea for his religious, social and artistic faith. The book was an amusing attack upon renaissance and recent building in which Welby dubbed Bath, Regent Street and St. Paul's as pagan. His own preference was for Christian building. In continuation of his condemnation of classic architecture, he proclaimed that the renaissance was alien and that the use of porticoes was wasteful of precious space, and false, in that its success involved resort to contorted symmetry and other artificial devices.

The technique used by the author to enforce his text was to provide contrasting illustrations of buildings intended to serve the same purpose in each of the two manners. In the selection of these, the scales were heavily weighted on the side of the Gothic. The same method is still frequently used by those who seek to persuade the reader that one set of pots and pans is better designed than another, but in 1837 it had the appeal of novelty.

The ideas at the root of Pugin's contentions were similar to those that Cobbett, Carlyle and others had voiced, namely that the restoration of the organisation and economy of the Middle Ages would make England merry again. Naturally it followed for an architect, like Welby Pugin, that the form of building co-incident with those halcyon days would be most appropriate for the day he visualised as to come. The effect of this propaganda and that of others had been that by the fifties, and Pugin's early death, revived Gothic had become for many the only dress for any building claiming to be architecture. These new pointed-arched structures had a familiar aspect that was disarming. The man in the street accepted the revival as natural, although he knew nothing about its causes. The works reminded him dimly of the parish church in the village he had quitted to better himself in the town. True there were diehards who practised in the Italian manner or its variants, but these were engaged in fighting a rearguard action.

Between the two contending parties in the battle of the styles, the Armstrongs of the profession made money building bonded stores, warehouses and mills, untroubled by any architectural assumption, so long as their " walls were alright and their construction generally good ". They were not as despicable as the " art " architects believed. In fact it was they who were extending the vernacular building and employing all manner of ingenious means to cope with the many unprecedented problems requiring solution. The large public were really indifferent—they left it to architects to tell them what was architecture and what was building—a distinction they were now persistently making.

This was the chaotic situation in which Edward found the profession he had entered. Here he was, engaged by his practical employer to provide the architecture his clients required. In most instances this consisted in adding some useless excrescences to an otherwise convenient building, but on occasion the matter went deeper.

Church dignitaries, bank directors, school managers, English gentlemen, were all apparently anxious that their environment should appear as if it had been built some time between the Conquest and the Tudors—with Victorian sanitation added. The impulses that actuated them were associative. The trouble was that associations might be satisfied in some other historic period at the self-same time or change suddenly in a few years, and it had become the architect's business as a student of such matter to provide the favoured setting. What was common to all of them, architects and laymen, was a felt dissatisfaction with their confused environment, and it was this that prompted them to dress it up in scenic trappings.

Now that Pugin was dead the leadership of the revival, if such it can be called, fell to George Gilbert Scott. Though a year older than Welby, he was as yet but slightly known. He was supported by Butterfield and George Edmund Street, young men who were advocates in their respective ways for revived Gothic. Eventually they were to be joined by younger men— James Brooks, G. F. Bodley, J. P. Seddon and William Burges, all of them older than Edward Godwin.

All of these were men of distinctive mind, and anything but opportunists. In the near future all of them were to design buildings having mediaeval inspiration, an issue which shows how strongly the current was running in the Gothic stream.

They had selected this manner from a conviction that through its potentialities a contemporary architecture would emerge. They adhered to this belief because they felt that their predecessors, who had toyed with several styles, had lacked sincerity.

These architects were those with whom in a few years Edward was to associate. At the moment the younger of them were commencing their independent careers.

Meantime he was completing his articles, and occupying his spare time in various forms of self-improvement, most of them being also pleasurable relaxations. In the autumn and winter evenings there was little entertainment for the youth of Bristol. They had to make it for themselves. True there was the Theatre Royal, and of this Edward was a devoted patron; indeed his visits to the theatre prompted him to take a lively interest in the plays of Shakespeare, so with his friend James Hine, the youth who had helped to measure Ancient Bristol for Mr. Burder, he commenced the study of the playwright's works. The two visited each other's homes in turn and methodically read aloud a play each week. They memorised much of the blank verse and discussed the play's themes endlessly, imagining themselves into the form of the characters they feigned in the back room of Earl's Mead where, beyond the snow-covered garden, ran the River Frome.

Like the rest, Edward was entertained by the books of the novelists, Scott, Dickens and Thackeray. He read all the stories he could obtain which they had written. The romance writing of the Middle Ages by Scott suited his mood, and rendered real to him the distant past ; Dickens was nearer, depicting amusingly the times his father had known ; Thackeray some of the elegances to which he aspired. Less usually, he enjoyed poetry, his favourites being Chaucer, Chatterton, Tennyson and Browning. Chaucer and Chatterton in particular. As was then the custom, he read the Bible from cover to cover.[1]

The marked omission from the programme of his reading was the classics, for none of the Greek or Roman writers were read by him during his adolescence, save some little translation he had been obliged to do at school.

It may appear as if he were unduly studious, but when it is recollected that there were few distractions, and that he was trying unaided to acquire the sort of background a university is designed to provide, his conduct was not unusual. All the diligent apprentices were burning the candle at both ends, or so it was afterwards said of them, and by them when they recalled their youth. It was not yet the fashion to aver that one had been a duffer at school.

Self-education is the most effective, its chief disadvantage, that it takes more time than that directed by others, being outweighed by the development through use of the faculties of apprehension. Nor did it interfere with his office training, for before he was eighteen he had become responsible for the design, drawings, specifications and superintendence of all the architectural work in progress at Armstrong's.

[1] *The British Architect*, 1880, p. 70.

B

CHAPTER II

THE MEDIAEVAL MASQUERADE

WHEN EDWARD became of age he left the office of Mr. Armstrong. Although at one time he admitted "That it was not such a bad training after all"—with the next breath he complained that he had not been properly recognised by his employer, his grievance being that although he did all the work, William Armstrong, who had never set eyes upon the drawings until he signed them, would not allow him to put his initials upon them. He used to say that he would have gladly served a longer term of pupilage if this privilege had been granted. He had overlooked the consequence for his parents who would have had to support him longer. The matter appears trivial, but in Edward's eyes it was serious, and bordered on forgery. That it really upset him is confirmed by the number of times in after life that he referred to the prohibition. Indeed, all his assistants were allowed to sign their names in full, when such a practice was not allowed by other architects.

Thus he parted from Mr. Armstrong. He had grown to be a slightly built, brown-eyed young man, inclined to be delicate. The Women, with whom he was a favourite, thought him very good looking and their admiration was repaid, for he could not resist feminine charm. He was undoubtedly gifted as an artist, and instinctively elegant in all matters of taste. This fastidious selection of suitable shapes was inherited from his ancestors who before the family became curriers had been potters, and his mother, who in the shadowy nature of her being contributed to his make-up the temperament of an introvert. His sister was similarly endowed. But at twenty-one he was uncertain of the direction in which his gifts were to be exercised. The need to secure a livelihood obscured his inner convictions which were subjective, critical, and based upon his own assessment of values. He was, as has been told, studious, eagerly searching for justification and precedent for his intuitions. To this end the written word had importance since there was no school where he could get guidance or receive criticism.

The experience he had had with William Armstrong gravely influenced his being, though as yet its marks were only recognisable in the self-centred assurance it had given him, that he could cope with everyday themes unaided. Later in life his early experience was apt to colour his judgement of others and to lead him to suspect the claims of the pretentious. On his own habits it had the effect that, in order to assure himself, he devoted an inordinate part of his time to the examination of authorities and the evidence of artifacts, merely for the confirmation or correction of his intuitions.

There is no doubt that he was an unusual young man. His familiarity with the Middle Ages, reminiscent of the genius Chatterton, was only realised by a few of his acquaintances. His social graces, however, were much easier to appreciate. He could talk intelligently about most things, books and plays, though he preferred one person as an audience rather than a crowd. He had an almost feminine interest in costume, he was musical and played the organ with feeling. All his interests were artistic. Even the long walks that he went, his only form of active recreation, had health or the search for beauty as their objective. With his career to make he had the optimism of youth, and believed that merit would not pass unnoticed or ability unemployed. He had, to support his optimism, the comforting philosophy of Samuel Smiles. It was his confidence that irritated others, who called it pride. Yet he never boasted, was quick to admit his mistakes, and did not consciously assume airs. To be misunderstood is the common fate of genius in a business community or of the superior at the hands of the inferior.

Full of hope he opened an office, near that of William Armstrong, at No. 1 Surrey Street and there stuck up his plate as an Architect and Surveyor. The rooms were small and unimpressive, the tenant very serious, over-anxious to show his father that he had not wasted his time.

It was fortunate for his peace of mind that soon after he had quitted Mr. Armstrong's employ he was commissioned to design a small school. Although he thought subsequently that the resulting building had little merit, a not uncommon sentiment of designers, he was proud that this, the first contract for which he was solely responsible, was completed without extras. In fact, the building actually cost between five and six pounds less than the accepted estimate, showing that the drawings and specification had been at any rate sufficiently comprehensive. The building, like every one of his early works, was Gothic. The fashionable architectural opinion of the time had got complete hold over him. He was nothing if not fashionable.

When his school was completed the people of Bristol did not hear of this economical accomplishment, nor did they, when they saw the building, realise the latent ability of the recent ghost of William Armstrong. They could hardly have been expected to make the discovery in so short an interval. The time when he essayed to start his career was unfavourable. People were too occupied in thinking and talking of the Crimean War, and soon after of Florence Nightingale and of the Mutiny in India, to trouble themselves about building anything. And when in 1857 the financial crisis knocked the bottom out of industrial enterprise in England, youth and business stagnation left Edward with time on his hands. Still never at a loss for something to do he helped a local architect, read his Shakespeare and visited the theatre. He had by importunity persuaded the editor of a local paper to accept and publish a series of criticisms of the plays performed in the Theatre Royal. This engagement allowed him to frequent the Theatre on the free list, and was an important factor in his education.

Meantime he was commissioned to design a few houses and to effect some alterations, none of which, however, afforded anything more than useful experience. There was nothing unusual in this, every architect commencing in practice has to endure the same indifference of the world as to his fate. Every young architect thinks he is being wronged. He was feeling depressed when at this moment of crisis his brother made a suggestion. This young man was already in practice as a Civil Engineer in the North of

Ireland and it looked ominously to Edward as if his father had been right in believing that engineering offered more scope than architecture. The suggestion, made in a letter from the Civil Engineer, was, that instead of waiting in Bristol for something to turn up, Edward should join him in Ireland for a month or two.

Edward did not hesitate, he packed up at once and went to visit his relative. At least it would be something to do, a fresh experience and, at the lowest valuation, a holiday. The idea in the mind of his brother was that the architect should help the engineer with the drawings for a proposed railway bridge which was to be constructed from a selected competitive design. Arrived in Ireland by the Dublin packet, the two young enthusiasts set to work on the plans for the project that was to win them fame and fortune, and then anxiously awaited the award.

They did not win!

They were keenly disappointed, for their hopes had been high. Edward meditated a return to England as had been his intention, but fate had other schemes in view, for some Irish friends of his brother seized the lucky chance of engaging his services, and asked him to design a small church. Nothing could have suited him better. Church design had been the subject to which, as a pupil, he had devoted the most study. His library, his sketch-books, his head were brimful of ideas.

The new building was to be erected at St. Johnston, County Donegal. The plan comprised nave, choir, transepts and porch. The exterior, a picturesque outline of high, steep roofs, was reminiscent of the ideals of his then beau-ideal of the profession, George Edmund Street. They had not met, but the young Edward had decided that of the architects then illustrating their work, Street was the most able. His admiration for the work of Street had been awakened by an illustration of the Theological College at Cuddesdon, Wheatley, Oxford, " a simple but picturesque pile of buildings, chiefly depending for effect on artistic proportions ". Simplicity and proportion were the attributes he believed necessary to achieve architecture. This was no small discovery by the young man from Bristol. Street was that perpetual hero of the young of the profession, " the hope of English architecture ".

The foundation stone of his Irish church was laid on the 4th April, 1857, when the architect was not yet twenty-four. A month later an illustration of the finished conception was printed in *The Builder*, first bringing the name of Edward Godwin to the notice of the outside world. It seemed that thus early his luck had turned.

It is a pleasurable experience to watch the realisation in material form of the ideas, originating in the mind, set out on paper. Edward enjoyed every day of his building's growth, and when the church was finished he was proud of his handiwork. The parishioners also were pleased, and considered that they had obtained one of the best churches in Northern Ireland. Over his conception Edward had every reason for satisfaction. As the first project of a young man it revealed distinctly the power of composition that was his gift. Perhaps he had succeeded in incorporating too much in too little ? It embodied too many parts for so modest a purpose.

He visited St. Johnston some years afterward when his good opinion was modified. He thought he could have selected his materials better, for those he had used had not toned to his liking. The detail, also, was hard and mechanical ; in truth it wore, he felt, marks of the engineer's outlook. The faults are those which one of his temperament naturally observed, and were the consequence of his association in Bristol with widely differing natures. The dream excelled the reality.

Before and during the time filled in building the Church of St. Johnston, Edward was occupied either in assisting his brother, or in designing and overseeing the erection of a number of small homesteads in the neighbourhood, fashioned in the regional vernacular manner, with the pigsty as part of the house. Their plan was very simple, consisting of a porch, a pantry, a pigsty, a living-room with a fire, on either side of which two small bedrooms were entered. They were not Gothic, save in the original sense of the term as uncouth.

In England some architects were experimenting in the same direction minus the pig. In Ireland young Edward had reached the conclusion independently that, to get the best out of the labour and craftsmanship of the rural operatives, and to provide a suitable building, it was advisable to utilise the traditional notions of accommodation, material and construction. Already some of the up-to-date landlords and architects had thrust villa architecture upon the Irish peasants, the resultant buildings looking and being absurdly out of place. They were too high and insufficiently weather-proof. That was what Edward thought—so, in the manner of Welby Pugin, he illustrated, by contrasting sketches of local and imported cottage designs, the unsuitability and inferiority of the latter. In all probability the culprits felt him to be young and presumptuous.

During this stay in Ireland he did not forget his antiquarian interests. He had never found any difficulty in employing his spare time, and while he had pursued knowledge for the disinterested pleasure of discovery, he had found that frequently the information collected could be subsequently applied. His measuring had been used in Bristol, and his church studies had helped him to design his own.

It is not surprising then that he should have been busy in a way that appeared of little moment to the spectator. Tramping in the rain to remote places, he made a collection of drawings of the Crosses of Donegal " extending from the earliest to the latest period and of all sizes from four inches to fourteen feet upwards ". The last were boundary marks. There was no accounting for the strange occupation of the English visitor. He was carefree and happy, and instead of staying in Ireland for two months he stopped for two years.

Eventually home called. It was time to attempt to resume practice in his birthplace before, through overlong absence, he should be forgotten. He recommenced at No. 1 Surrey Street, Bristol.

The stay in Ireland had matured him ; he was less youthfully assertive, and better looking than ever. His health had improved. His life there had been more natural, more varied, and entirely new. His occasional returns to Bristol had been in the character of holidays. As to architecture, he had reached these conclusions —first, that construction was important ; second, that proportion made building art ; last, that the vernacular or non-literate was not to be despised, for it included consideration of texture as one of its characteristics. It was his intention to co-ordinate these realisations as a whole on the first favourable opportunity.

The most immediate chance he had was provided by a new warehouse required in Merchant Street, Bristol. It was this unexpected commission that had influenced his decision to return. As, at this date, he was an ambitious " Goth " his elevation was in this manner—there had been similar stores in the Middle Ages—so why not now ?

The warehouse was built upon the site of an eighteenth-century dwelling-house destroyed by fire in 1856. " The new building was divided into three stories, running the entire depth of the premises, and communicating upon the ground floor, with a glass-roofed hauling way. . . ." The elevation to Merchant Street was " Early English in character " and was in part composed of some fragments of wrought stone found on the site, which ad-joined Bristol Castle. The walls were built in coursed rubble, with Pennant jambs, piers and bands, and Bath stone arches, cills and strings. The composition of the elevation was symmetrical and save for the plate tracery in the upper windows was devoid of excrescences. The building is interesting as a stage in his progress towards a solution of the warehouse elevation in the fashionable Gothic. His Merchant Street warehouse was a novelty—*The Builder* was constrained to remark on the suitability or adapt-ability of the style to the use to which it had been put—" the illustration shows how easily Gothic architecture may be applied to a structure of this class ".[1]

He found, however, that during his absence from England, fashion in building had once more turned for inspiration in another direction. It was necessary to change the language in which he was to express himself. English Gothic was out of favour.

It appeared that a book, the first volume of which had been issued in 1851, the year of the Great Exhibition, *The Stones of Venice* by John Ruskin, had altered the course of the Gothic revival. Even Mr. Street was deflected. Before he had gone to Ireland, Edward had read Ruskin's earlier book, *The Seven*

[1]*The Builder*, October, 30th, 1858, p. 719.

Lamps of Architecture, but now all his friends told him that he must read *The Stones*. Opinions as to its value differed. Some readers said that it was a jumble of truth and fallacy set out in eloquent prose ; others complained that they could not understand the writer ; but all were none the less agreeable that his dicta be tested in building.

In these circumstances, the only choice open was to start on his own voyage of discovery and read the book ; so he bought a set and commenced a laborious examination of its tenets.

Less reluctantly he resumed his visits to the Theatre Royal with critical interest. For him the scenery was seldom in accord with the scene or the costume with the character. The use he made of his childhood familiarity with Planché's illustrations was to point out the errors in the dress of the players, and for the background of building, room or furniture, he was fortified in his comments by his recent practical experiences. There was plenty of scope for this kind of comment despite the meticulous accuracy with which both Planché and Charles Kean were deliberately staging plays.

Possibly unfamiliar with Kean's fastidious accuracy, Edward wrote to the actor to point out some supposed error. Kean replied politely, asking him to get in contact with his scene painter, though he did not promise any amendment. Now that he was back in Bristol, the newspapers resumed their publication of his unusual comments on the décor at the Theatre Royal as a regular feature. For from the first his regard was visual. Prone to put too much stress on accuracy he was not concerned for the text of the play, except when it gave, as it frequently did, some clue to the colour of the costume, the kind of dress, or the motions of the actor. He was interested in the acting ; inflection affected him more than words.

It was during this second attempt to establish a business, that he made friends with William Burges, a Londoner, and an architect who had already distinguished himself by winning the Lille Cathedral competition. Godwin's notice of Burges was attracted by an illustration of a fountain in Gloucester that Burges had designed. On seeing this design Edward impetuously resolved that when next he went to London he would call and introduce himself.

Shortly afterwards this wish was realised. Up the stairs of 15 Buckingham Gate he climbed in search of the stranger whose acquaintance he sought. Knocking on the door—" I introduced myself; he was hospitable, poured wine into a silver goblet of his own design, and placed bread upon the table. With a few words we ate and drank." The meeting, which took place in a narrow bed-sitting-room that communicated with the outer office, was a serious, ceremonious encounter of two men, like-minded, but of different circumstances.

William Burges (1827–1881) was a wealthy young man. Though older than his visitor, he had only recently commenced independent practice as an architect—after a pupilage with Blore, an assistantship with Digby Wyatt, and a partnership with Henry Clutton. It was with the last of these that he had won the Lille award. He was small as men go, and his turn of mind was humorous. He talked rapidly, with his head on one side. " His temper was certainly volatile."[1] To his friends he was affectionately known as " Billy ". He had a vein of simplicity in his make-up which led some people to take playful advantage of his convictions. Godwin treated him seriously, for Burges was unquestionably an able scholar, an extraordinarily inventive creator of pseudo-mediaeval whimsies, altogether an astonishingly able exponent of revived Gothic. In many respects the two young men were in agreement as to the aims of the artist. They were both escapists engaged in an attempt to bring back beauty into their environment; their talents were very similar, and although both were Gothic enthusiasts, yet neither was without sympathy for Greek art. Burges, in fact, had recently visited Athens. "It was not until I was actually on the spot," he said, "that I understood how beautiful Greek Architecture was."[2] Both were draughtsmen gifted beyond the ordinary, each with an individual style. Their similarities extended to their common interest in the theatre. One of the plans they spontaneously agreed upon at this meeting was to design a theatre in collaboration, because in their

[1] M. B. Adams, R.I.B.A. Journal, July 27th, 1912, p. 643.
[2] The Art Journal, 1886, p. 170.

opinion all the theatres they knew were obsolete. On this first encounter they discovered that they had different views on what passed for beauty, particularly in the realm of colour. Burges was all for primary colours while Godwin favoured neutral or half tones. In Edward's view all Burges' work was too heavy, or clumsy, and he told him as much. They debated the subject at length. Fortunately Burges was one of the few men who could discuss aesthetics and meet with disagreement and opposition without bearing any sense of injury afterward. Other men got hot and bothered. Edward formed the opinion that Burges' exaggerations of the profiles of mouldings and preferences for vivid colours were due to short-sightedness which prevented him from appreciating their effect upon persons of normal vision. " I spoke in no uncertain tones in those days when neither of us had much to do."[1]

Although he had not much to do—he was restoring the south porch of St. Mary, Redcliffe, a job which should have flattered his vanity—Edward had been sufficiently confident to become engaged to the daughter of a clergyman. It has not been possible to discover how or where they met. It may have been during the brief interval when he was assisting an unidentified architect in the South of England, to which experience he referred years later, or in Ireland when, on a holiday in August 1859, he revisited St. Johnston. Nor can more be said about the young lady than that she was a few years older than her lover and is said to have been highly educated and brilliant. What is known, however, is that on 1st November 1859 Edward married Miss Sarah Yonge, the daughter of the Rev. William Clarke Yonge of Henley. The ceremony was performed by the curate, the Rev. William Jebb Few, in the Parish Church of Henley-on-Thames, when the bride was given away by her father in the presence of her relatives. Though his parents were still living they are not known to have been at the wedding. After the honeymoon the couple set up house in Brighton Villa, Richmond Road, Upper Montpelier, Bristol.

Back in Bristol, Godwin resumed his analysis of *The Stones of Venice*, not without hope that he would gain something from the book's difficult pages. Ruskin had tried his best to be methodical, yet the division into chapters, sections and more sub-divisions made it no more easy to follow the argument. It seemed that there were merits in the Ducal Palace that had hitherto escaped notice, and that the arts working as a team could produce magnificent works. The latter suggestion at all events was worth trying, so Edward lent the book to a mason who was working for him—as well start early to found a team. As for himself, he resolved to put the precepts of *The Stones of Venice* to the test.

Northampton needed a new Town Hall. Designs were called for in competition from architects, and Edward decided that this contest presented a favourable opportunity to try his hand.

Although the bridge in Ireland had left him rather sceptical about competitions, the ardent disciple determined to put into the design the whole of his new-found mentor's suggestions. Now that he was married, it was more than ever necessary that he should justify himself. Working single-handed day and night, he at length completed his drawings. All over the country other hopeful competitors had been similarly engaged, and in all forty sets of designs were submitted for judgement by nearly as many expectant architects.

Some of the competitors were fearful that the selection of the successful design (a task that the Corporation had reserved for themselves) would be unfair. They wrote to the building papers suggesting that a professional assessor should be consulted. It was late in the day to make such a proposal ; properly, that should have been made before entering for the contest.

In February 1861 the whole of the forty designs were exhibited to the Councillors, who in their wisdom selected six of them as meeting with their approval. In deference to the letters in the press, they resolved that the six sets should be submitted to an architect, with a request for his considered report. They chose as assessor Mr. William Tite, M.P. (afterward Sir William), a devotee of the Italian renaissance manner of building who was specialising in the design of railway stations.

. Tite took some time to consider the submissions before he made his report. Of the six he had examined, he recommended three for further consideration by the Council. These he placed in numerical order—indicating his own preference. In his report he explained the merits and demerits of them all. After reflecting over the subject, the Council by twelve votes to three selected the design endorsed *Non Nobis Domini*. This design had been Tite's second preference, his first had been a scheme of renaissance character.

Of the drawings placed second by Tite, signed *Non Nobis Domini* by the author, the assessor remarked:

" In this design the position of the hall on the ground floor seems to me to be much more desirable than the one suggested in the design last noticed; but in other respects, the plan is generally not so convenient as No. 1 and it is to be remarked that no provision whatever has been made for the Museum, required under article 20 of your instructions. No doubt this omission was accidental, and it could easily be remedied. . . . The sessions court would be, however, very convenient, and it solves the problem of extension very satisfactorily.

" As to the elevation towards St. Giles Square, I would suggest that the slender columns bearing statues under niches might very advantageously be omitted; and that the dormer windows in the roof are needlessly prominent.

" There is, however, a very remarkable degree of talent in the management of the style adopted; and if this design were carried into effect—it would be an ornament to your town."

The final selection was left by Mr. Tite in the hands of the Council. He advised them to be guided in their choice by a consideration of local requirements. When the envelope endorsed *Non Nobis Domini* was opened " the architect was found to be Mr. E. W. Godwin ".[1]

Ever since the original choice of the six sets of designs had been made, Godwin, with the others selected, had known that he might eventually be fortunate. He had been in an agony of suspense. When at long last he learned of his success he was very elated. Small wonder, for the building was an important Town Hall, with a frontage of eighty feet, and a depth of one hundred and eighty. To these dimensions he had added a tower one hundred

[1] *The Builder*, April 27th, 1861, p. 282.

and ten feet high. He had pitted his ability and Ruskin's views against the Kingdom and had triumphed. Since he was only twenty-seven years old, he felt himself young enough to anticipate a future. Architecture was not after all so disappointing a calling.

Burges wrote his congratulations and Ruskin sent several letters of advice; the author was as much gratified as the architect. Bristol felt proud and Sarah Godwin was happy.

Then the real business commenced. All the working drawings and documents had to be drafted. When at length they were ready for signature he took them with him to Northampton to lay before the City Fathers.

The conference was opened by one of the members of the Council, himself an architect, commenting on the drawings—" they are very fine, no doubt, but I should like to see all the details of that carving and of the figures drawn to a large scale."

The critical councillor was evidently anxious to impress his fellow members by his knowledge at the expense of an anxious young man. Edward promised to make the drawings suggested —they would in any event have to be made.

Next came the specification. An alderman, who by the way was in the iron trade, objected to the insertion of the names of the men to be employed to forge the ironwork and to sculpt the stones. This protest was awkward and unexpected. Edward suddenly realised " that he had made a mistake in not considering the local tradesmen ". He decided reluctantly to give way on the ironwork, of which there was not much. But as to the carving, " I would not give up my carving man, who was my carver at the time. I had educated him. He had worked for me in the West of England. He knew what I required. Moreover he had studied Ruskin, which was an important matter, because the building was entirely founded upon *The Stones of Venice*."

The team must be kept in being at all costs. The whole future of architecture was bound up in the unity of the arts. In desperation he pleaded to be allowed to retain the man he had nominated ; he relied upon him to interpret his drawings of the figures. The mason could not be abandoned. Eventually the

[1] *The British Architect*, November 29th, 1878.

alderman gave way; thus much to the architect's relief the engagement of the Ruskinian carver was approved, and the critic even allowed him to appoint as ironworker the man of his choice. The tension was relaxed.

The fulfilment of his promise to detail the figures of the kings and prelates which ranged across the front elevation was not so easy. Although he had copied Planché's figures and costumes as a boy, Edward had not yet drawn much from life.

In the end, however, assisted by reference to illustrations, he made a full size drawing of one of the group—Richard Coeur de Lion—that satisfied the Committee and the architect councillor who considerately excused him the immediate drawing of the rest. There were effigies of St. George, St. Michael, Henry III, Edward I, Edward IV, Henry VII and Queen Victoria on the elevation. Outside and inside there was much more sculpture representing scenes and persons connected with the history of Northampton. The sculptor about whom there had been so much discussion was Boulton of Worcester.

The building of the Town Hall proceeded smoothly over the following three years, its supervision entailing very frequent visits to the city. It was opened on May 17th, 1864, having been built without any deviation from the original competition drawings. The plan was a good one, so good that it was appropriated by the winning competitor in another competition without acknowledgement. All the furniture and decorations were designed by the architect and if anything were wrong the fault was his. When, at last, the whole was finished (it cost £20,917 3s. 11d.), the people of Northampton were proud of their Town Hall. Ruskin wrote expressing his approval.

So soon as Godwin saw his completed work without any scaffolding, he noticed some defects—" the first error that struck me was this. There was a string course which divided the building into two, and I had built the wall above the string course in a line with that below the string course. That was by no means an uncommon error, and now mark what happened. Up above the string course there was a series of statues standing on pillars, and those pillars projecting from the wall. The result was that to the end of its existence, the upper storey was top heavy. The mass looked as if it leaned forward. Had the upper part been set back a trifle the imperfection would have been optically corrected ".

If the vertical section had been insufficiently considered, the horizontal compensated for that oversight. " Ruskin was in a measure responsible for it, and it was good. The façade was divided into seven bays. No doubt at first sight the seven arches appear to be all of about the same span ; but I had read what Ruskin said about the charming building produced by having a series of arches of different widths. He went into ecstasies over the west front of St. Mark's, Venice, because they were of different widths, producing a beautiful wave-like harmony."[1]

This irregularity of setting out is one of the sources of the charm of mediaeval work, the importance of which had been missed by the early Gothic revivalists. It was this defect in his tracery at St. Johnston that Edward had felt as mechanical.

Although the people of Northampton were gratified, no one, except the Mayor, then asked him to act as their architect. They felt diffident about approaching him with their trivial schemes. His Worship, however, made of sterner stuff, had engaged Edward to design him two houses. When afterward questioned about them, Edward remarked, with a trace of amusement, " They were in fact *The Stones of Venice* all over again ".

Northampton Town Hall impressed Godwin's architect contemporaries and gained for him a place in Charles Eastlake's *History of the Gothic Revival*, the book about the movement that was published shortly after the Town Hall had been completed. Eastlake was an architect, and at this time the Secretary of the Royal Institute of British Architects. Needless to tell, the historian recognised his source of inspiration. " It is impossible to examine this front," he wrote, " without feeling that at this period the designer was strongly influenced by the prevalent taste for Italian Gothic and by the principles of design which Mr. Ruskin had lately advocated."[2]

Of its manner, the building is undoubtedly the finest in England ; the detailing of the work is exquisite, the composition

[1] *The British Architect*, November 29th, 1878.
[2] *The Gothic Revival*, C. L. Eastlake, p. 358.

21 Portland Square, Bristol.

WAREHOUSE, 104 STOKES CROFT, BRISTOL

of that part of the building flanking the tower, beautiful. This was the extent of the original conception, the rest was added later (1892) by E. W. Holding, a local man. The defects to which Edward referred are barely apparent. If the building has any fault, it lies in the rather too close spacing of the centres of the arcading as seen in perspective. It is not difficult to realise the thrill of pleasure the sight of the Town Hall evoked when fresh and lovely. Other cities might boast of bigger buildings but Northampton owned the best.

CHAPTER III

21 PORTLAND SQUARE

IN 1862, when Northampton Town Hall was in course of
construction and providing Edward with an assured income,
moreover when it seemed as if its successful completion
would lead to continuous employment, he removed with his
wife to No. 21 Portland Square, Bristol, which was conveniently
situated in a fashionable locality and was possessed of architectural character. He was moving up in the world. The house
was on the corner of the Square adjoining Bishop Street, separated
by three houses from the Church of St. Paul's, with its Wren-
like Gothic tower and astonishing composite plaster interior.
They—the Godwins—went there on Sunday.

The church had been consecrated by Bishop Christopher
Wilson, in 1792, and so out of compliment it was flanked by
Bishop Street on the left and Wilson Street on the right hand.

No. 21 was a large stone-built house with the windows, on
each of the five floors, fronting to the garden of the Square which
was enclosed by a palisade of iron with gates and lamps, altogether an elegant eighteenth-century town house, one of the
several similar houses surrounding the four sides of the quiet
Square.

On the decoration and furnishing of his new home he spent
much time and thought. It was to be entirely to his taste and that
meant that it would differ from the familiar interiors of his
Victorian neighbours. From the outside it looked much like all
the other houses. Yet it differed in one small particular from his
own design—his door-knocker. His door-knocker, a ball on a
chain, excited the attention of the passer-by to such a degree that
the young wags of the district made a practice of removing
specimens as a souvenir of their evening escapades. It was

common knowledge among them that Godwin was odd—and his knocker was testimony to his oddity. He was far too brainy.

Some months earlier William Morris had completed his Red House at Upton, Kent. He had then been troubled by the same problem as now faced Edward, how to furnish. Morris had chosen a mediaeval setting of his own and his pre-Raphaelite friends' devising, this because he found it impossible to furnish his home from the goods for sale in the trade. Not so Edward.

His scheme consisted in painting the walls of his rooms in plain colours, hanging thereon a few Japanese prints—then a rarity in England—laying some Persian rugs on the bare floors and completing the decoration with carefully selected antique furniture. Save for the oriental woodcuts it was a reversion to the taste of the eighteenth century in keeping with the building.

Middle-class Bristol did not approve. His interior decoration was thought by his neighbours to provide evidence of eccentricity; they could not understand anyone who appeared to regard beauty before upholstered comfort as other than peculiar.

They were unused to anything so Spartan; simplicity they equated with poverty. In truth such a scheme was unfamiliar, and in opposition to the prevalent taste of the period. Possibly it was his interest in the art of Japan, his liking for asymmetrical arrangements, or his stress on health, that motivated his actions. There was no contemporary precedent, though there were some similar interiors in the town and country houses of the nobility which had escaped the attention of the commercial decorator. From now on Godwin was felt to be a little queer. Not only did he read Shakespeare, but he was said to dress in period costume when at home.

Some people, however, had confidence in him. Rather poetically he was now (1862) employed in the design of extensive additions to Highbury Chapel, the building which, as a boy, had attracted him toward architecture. Butterfield, the first architect, had become fearful to work for the non-conformists, and had had to do penance for his only transgression. The trustees were then free to engage another architect. Edward's addition to the building consisted in the provision of an apse, a semi-transept, the tower and lecture hall. Their design pays some deference to Butterfield's original building as indeed it should—yet it differs in that such tracery as is contained in the windows is slightly stronger in section, the tower is banded in wrought stone more like some of the first architect's later work. The stair tower in dressed stone—at the time of erection somewhat stark —has since been harmonised with the whole by time.

In Bristol also, at 104 Stokes Croft, he was building another warehouse. The elevation of this was a marked advance on the earlier essay in Merchant Street—only the materials, Pennant stone and Bath stone in arches and bands, were similar. It was three storeys in height, divided on the ground floor into five bays by arches, and on the first and second floors into ten windows. The composition of this simple front is subtle, the selection of the stone, its coursing and dressing reveal the refinement of perception to which he had attained. It is a master-work of its kind. Lower down the same street he built two shops, Nos. 74 and 76. This time he used red brick over a Gothic ground floor. The two upper storeys—the topmost partly in the roof—were terminated at the eaves in an elaborate corbelled brick cornice. The Gothic shop-fronts, which, it is said, were charming, have been removed; the upper part appears to have been an attempt to re-establish a brick vernacular.

Let the layman think what he liked, Godwin could not well be ignored by his profession. Architects are tolerant, thus in June 1862 he was elected a Fellow of the Bristol Architectural Society, and on the same day he was appointed Honorary Secretary and Librarian, and elected as one of the delegates to attend a meeting of the Architectural Alliance at the Architectural rooms in Conduit Street.

The Bristol Society had been founded in 1850, and one of its first acquisitions had been a copy of Burder, Hine and Godwin's *Antiquities of Bristol*. The Alliance had been formed as a means of associating provincial architectural societies with each other, and with the Royal Institute of British Architects, at whose headquarters—the old house designed by James Wyatt—they met. Their objectives were defence and defiance.

Next month Edward attended the conference in London, and the following day reported the proceedings to his Society. He had the prestige pertaining to the winner of an open competition. Moreover he was bursting with enthusiasm and constructive ideas

As soon as he had been installed as secretary, Edward, like a new broom, began to sweep clean. He joined in all their activities, and was constantly suggesting others for their acceptance. When they went on visits to the neighbouring places, it was he who acted as guide. He showed them over Clapton Church, that had been a haunt of his student days, and about which he knew all that there was to be known. More ambitiously he conducted the members over Exeter and Gloucester Cathedrals. At the meetings he read a number of papers, some the composition of absent or bashful members. He was a practised reader, and whenever they were, for any reason, short of a paper, and that was often, he stepped into the absentee's place and gave a talk of his own. He had plenty of material upon which to draw, in the local antiquities—the Abbey of St. Augustine or Bristol Cathedral. His lecture on the Cathedral was afterwards published as a pamphlet illustrated by five plates showing the successive phases of the development. The Irish Crosses that he had sketched and measured formed the theme of a further talk. He was the ideal secretary, the man who runs the organisation while the rest of the members look on and grumble. He grumbled himself, chiefly at the unhelpfulness of the members.

All the interests of his youth had persisted into his manhood : music—in the form of organ playing, to practice which he had built an organ in his home ; Shakespeare—the two original enthusiasts had been joined by a number of friends who met regularly to read the plays ; literature—he read omniferously and collected rare books ; and the theatre with its many facets. He and his wife frequented the old Theatre Royal with its highly-decorated Corinthian auditorium. Afterwards he wrote, for the press, his commentary of the performance. He made a profession of his pleasure.

Still it was not all pleasure. The occupation had its risks. One evening an actor, connected with the management, whom Godwin had criticised candidly in his weekly *Jottings*, called round at Portland Square, and was shown in by the unsuspecting maid to Edward, who was in the dining-room dressed in a costume as

Henry V. Suddenly the visitor produced a horsewhip and, without warning, lashed at Godwin vigorously as he retreated before him round the table ; clad, as he was, in hose he could offer little resistance. The affair was hushed up at the time, but many years after Edward ruefully referred to the assault, seemingly suggesting that some such incident had happened not once, but twice!

Nevertheless, the dangerous calling of dramatic critic had its compensations—for when he praised he made friends for life, and the approved actors carried his commendation—clipped from the newspaper—about with them to show to the sceptical, until the cuttings were worn out. They thought the writer a fine fellow.

In the winter of 1861, when engaged in this journalistic work, he had singled out for praise the remarkable performance of a child actress as Puck. The little girl was called Ellen Terry, and had first appeared five years before at the Prince's Theatre as Mamillius in *The Winter's Tale* with her elder sister Kate. The Terrys were not unknown to him, for Edward had earlier met their parents when they had visited Bristol. He had already noted Kate Terry and Marie Wilton as actresses of distinction likely to become great.

Now, this year 1862, the two girls, Kate and Ellen, had joined the stock company of Mr. Chute at the Bristol Theatre, where Kate Terry, though only a young girl, was the leading lady. The two children, their parents, and their younger brothers and sisters lodged in Queen's Square, a short walk from the Theatre. They were much sought after by the young bloods of Bristol, most of whom were anxious to be introduced to the pretty and attractive sisters. Since they were jealously guarded by their mother, zest was added to the quest. The beaux loitered under the elms in the Square, or by the railings fronting their apartments, in hopeful anticipation of an encounter, and if not there, then at the traditional trysting place—the stage door.

The company were playing in Shakespearian repertory, and it seemed to Godwin appropriate to ask the Terry girls to join the reading party in Portland Square. If need be, he was fortified by his long acquaintance with the theatre management, his well-known interest in everything to do with the stage, his friendship with their mother and father, and his declared admiration of the young ladies' talents. He asked the girls to come and help the enthusiastic amateurs. Mr. and Mrs. Terry giving their permission, Kate and Ellen came as guests to Portland Square at the other side of the city. It was to be a fateful meeting.

Ellen, the younger of the two girls was not yet fifteen years old. She was a fair-haired and lively child, and born to the stage; she graced without apparent effort the small parts in which she was cast. It was a change and relief from life in lodgings to have found a friendly host in Bristol.

When Ellen saw the inside of his home she was charmed. The decoration and furnishing were unlike anything she had seen in any other private house or on the stage. Her host and his wife impressed her equally as unique—" Its master and mistress made me think."[1] They were so interesting and clever, the sort of people she had longed to know. The house was not queer, it was beautiful. The other people she met there were memorable. Seated in his elegant room, each with the play to be read in his hand, were James Hine and William Burges—the jolly little architect from London. He, moreover, was a confirmed theatregoer. There was also another architect in the party, Henry Crisp, a striking-looking man with a florid complexion, wearing a jacket without lapels. He was not only a friend of the Godwins but also of her family. The comedy *The Midsummer Night's Dream* formed the evening's entertainment. Chute was intending to open the Theatre Royal, Bath, in March 1863, with the *Dream* and had chosen Ellen for the role of Titania—the Queen of the Fairies—so the evening was helpful as well as happy.

When the ladies and the rest had been seen home, the two architects Burges and Godwin sat talking until the early hours of the next day before they went to bed. The reason for the meeting was that Burges had a cathedral to build at Finbar, and every time he visited Ireland he broke his journey to spend a day or two with the Godwins, when, if a meeting of the circle was due, he was inveigled into reading Shakespeare before taking the steam-packet to the island.

At the week-end the girls and Godwin called on their friend

[1] Ellen Terry, *Memoirs*, 1933, p. 37.

Crisp at his cottage, the Cherry Orchard, Coombe Dingle, Westbury-on-Trym. It was a simple little place with a straight flight of stairs opposite the front door, with a handrail on each side wall. To Henry Crisp's astonishment, Ellen stood on the top landing at the bedroom floor level, took hold of the handrail and jumped from the landing to the mat on the ground floor at one bound. She was an active young lady. Crisp thought her to be, then and always, adorable.

In the new year, in anticipation of her appearance at Bath, Edward could not resist the chance offered to put into practice his ideas of costume. Together, he and Ellen set about the making of a Grecian dress for her part. He designed the whole, cut out the material and helped her to do the sewing; finally wetting and wringing it out when finished, so that it unfolded, "all crinkled and clinging", in the real ancient manner.[1] It was good fun. Best of all, their combined work was a great success, the dress was much admired when Titania wore it on the stage.

The all too brief run of *A Midsummer Night's Dream* came to an end when the two young ladies had to leave Bath in order to fulfil an engagement to appear at the Haymarket. The Terry family returned to London.

When his new friends had left Edward resumed his old life; in April he was re-elected Honorary Secretary of the Bristol Society. In the summer he went to France for a holiday with his wife. His friend Burges had talked so much about the superior virtues of French Gothic and told everybody that they should study the Sainte Chapelle, Paris, that Edward was persuaded that he had better go and see its splendours for himself.

Northampton Town Hall was progressing toward the stage when the interior could be decorated and furnished and did not require so much of his attention. In any event he needed and had earned a holiday. Amiens, Paris and Chartres were his chosen route, having been suggested to him as holding the culmination of continental Gothic and as being easily accessible. He intended his holiday to be a complete change, and in contrast to his previous habit he sketched nothing, took no measurements, and during the whole tour only made one water-colour. He was pleasantly

[1]Ellen Terry, *Memoirs*, 1933, p. 38.

lazy, merely sitting in the shade of the buildings upon the
structure of which he reflected. It was a lovely summer and he
idled to some purpose.

On his return, in order to give himself more time to attend
to his own affairs, he resigned his secretaryship of the Bristol
Society. He continued, however, his membership, indeed he
closed the year by writing a paper that was read in his absence,
through illness, by the new secretary, Phipps. The subject he
had chosen was *The Sister Arts*. Unfortunately no record of
this lecture has been found. The unity of the arts under the
architect had been the theme of frequent conversations with
Burges. It was, moreover, implicit in the team working together,
the combination he had endeavoured to realise at Northampton.
In effect it implied the enlargement of the scope of the architect.
The designer of the whole should, he thought, be the author of
the parts. The notion was not new; it had been carried out by
Kent and Adam, to name but two of the several architects who
had persuaded their patron that the building and its equipment
should be a unity—only to be realised if designed by the same
hand. The setting, that is the garden about the house, claimed
equally the architect's guidance. The industrial age had led
to the segregation of the designer, who worked now only upon
one form of commodity. The effect was the discordance of
object with object and of subject with setting.

In his own person and practice Godwin tried to unite all the
arts; he disliked the title architect as too limited. He preferred
the wider term artist, as all-embracing and yet selective. The
Morris firm were actuated by similar ideas. Godwin differed from
William Morris and Philip Webb in that his furniture design
was less archaic even when based on mediaeval types. His private
preferences were entirely at variance, as was obvious at once to
any visitor to his house in Portland Square. There Edward could
be heard to exclaim that he " did not wish to eat his dinner in a
chair suited to Edward the Confessor ". Morris, on the other
hand, was apeing King Arthur's domestic arrangements. Both
of them had yet far to go. To those who only knew Northampton
it was not apparent that they differed. True the entire building
with its sculpture, metalwork, furniture and decoration had

emanated from his brain and was almost as related to the past as anything by William Morris. In that building the manner had been forced upon him by the pressure of time, but even so he had given the fittings a personal interpretation. The Gothic revivalists could not yet accuse him of public heresy—though they must have found his furniture questionable, but then, life had moved on since the fourteenth century.

He was supremely confident in his own capacity. If a man was an artist there was no limit to his creative powers. Already he had claimed the right to design furniture and to decorate the walls and floors as the province of the architect, as well as to design costumes and make them; to act and to criticise acting, costume and scenery; to lead and direct all these activities in the present, and to theorise and talk about the same in the past. Although many people ascribed this versatility to eccentricity they were obliged to admit that he was extremely capable. Moreover, when called upon to define in what direction, other than that of superior ability, he was peculiar, they were at a loss. His conversation was unaffected. His voice clear, handwriting cursive and most pleasant—gave not the least indication of anything but a sure sense of form and arrangement. The phrasing of his writings revealed a logical, accurate thinker. He was most equable under trying conditions. Business Bristol decided that the artist was a practical man—though he did read Shakespeare and sew costumes. It was recognised that he was getting on in the world, and that he was bringing Bristol into some prominence in architecture.

Unfortunately his health was uncertain and his work was interrupted by periodic breakdowns, the cause of which his doctor never recognised. Well or ill, he had a good friend in Henry Crisp—an architect whose temperament and talents were the complement of his own.

It was to Crisp that he turned for help when unwell, when away from Bristol, or on holiday.

Henry Crisp was the son of Thomas Skeffe Crisp, the Head of Bachelors College, Bristol, who had brought him up very strictly. As a youth he had been articled to Foster and Wood, and was now in practice on his own account at 28 Corn Street. Crisp was

a bachelor and rode to hounds, a recreation that proved his un-
doing, for a year from this time he met a widow in the hunting
field—and married a Tartar. This lady—Mrs. Niblett—had two
sons and a daughter by her first marriage.

Henry Crisp was a kindly man—unluckily he had a strawberry-
like skin. He used to jest about this disfigurement, telling that—
" one day, returning to the office, I asked the office boy, ' Has
anyone called ? '

" ' Yes, sir.'

" ' Did he leave his name ? '

" ' No, sir.'

" ' What was he like ? '

" ' Like you, sir, all sort of red and spotty like.' I knew then
that the caller was my brother, Dr. Crisp of Keynsham."

It was hardly any surprise, therefore, when, in January 1864,
Godwin and Crisp decided to enter into partnership : Edward
intending to concentrate upon competitions and visits to the
work in progress ; Crisp to devote his time to the letter-writing,
valuation, negotiations in Bristol, and the smaller works.

Crisp left his office in Corn Street, Godwin gave up the
Surrey Street address, and the firm opened an office at Godwin's
house, 21 Portland Square. The arrangement was an economy
and a convenience. The house was larger than was needed
by the Godwins as Edward was frequently away, and since
Mrs. Godwin was ailing, it was convenient that there should
be somebody at call about the house.

Just before the formal partnership was entered into, they had
submitted unsuccessfully two designs for Malvern College.
In partnership they were engaged on a house for Mr. Fuller at
Lansdown. Since they were otherwise rather slack, the partners
decided to enter for another competition.

A town hall was wanted for Congleton in Cheshire, the
accommodation required being a court, an Assembly Room to
seat 1,000, and a Market Hall. The whole was a much smaller
project than that at Northampton. The premium offered was the
absurdly small sum of £25, but this was eventually increased as
the result of a protest by the Architectural Alliance, which thus
early justified its establishment. Their protest was supported

by a spate of letters in the building papers. This matter settled, the competitors prepared for the fray.

For a number of reasons Godwin decided to give his design a French flavour; he was fresh from the study of examples; French Gothic was growing in professional favour; the Lille competition had given this twist to the thought of architects, and now seven years later it had seeped through. The recent publication of Viollet-le-Duc's Dictionary had made readily available a mass of technical information on the subject; two rising architects, Norman Shaw and Eden Nesfield, had had books of sketches of French examples printed; G. E. Street was exploiting French outline, and pedants declared that it was from France that the essentials of Gothic art had come to England. Turning over these facts in his mind, it seemed to him highly probable that the assessor would look for something French in order to justify his selection as a fashionable architect. Ruskin was out of date.

Crisp ordered a set of *Specimens of Early French Architecture,* only recently published by R. J. Johnson, from Mr. Birbeck of Birmingham. Godwin wrote to the promoters :

" 21 Portland Square,
" Jan. 27th, 1864.

" We shall feel obliged if you will give us information on the following points.

    1st. Are views admitted; if so may they be coloured or must they, like the elevations, be drawn only in sepia or indian ink ?

    2nd. Is the 3rd line of the 11th clause of the Conditions to be applied in all cases, that is in the event of a design by an architect in established practice being selected, or is it only intended as a protection in the event of a design by a young and inexperienced man being selected.

" We are, Sir, Yours obediently,

" GODWIN & CRISP.

" J. Walker Esq."

His mind satisfied on these points, Edward entered the contest wholeheartedly. This time he was relieved by a partner and had the help of a pupil.

In the meantime his mind had been active upon other matters —the education of the architect.

The claim of an architect to design the whole of the furnishings and fabric of his building, required, if it were to be justified, that he should be trained, from his entry into the profession, to perform his self-imposed tasks. In an endeavour to discover the competent members of the profession, and to confer upon the selected their diploma the Royal Institute had, in 1861, established a voluntary Architectural Examination. The subject interested him sufficiently to provoke him to write to the President of the Bristol Society of Architects the following self-explanatory letter :

" March 2nd, 1864.

" My dear Mr. Gabriel,

" As the state of my health will not permit me to be present at the meeting of the Society of Architects tonight, may I be allowed to call the attention of the general body to the report of the Hon^y. Sec^y. of the Royal Institute of British Architects on the voluntary Architectural Examination for 1864 just issued by the Institute and which I have requested my friend Mr. Crisp to lay upon the table.

" It must be very gratifying to you all to find one of our own student members on the list of successful candidates and I sincerely hope Mr. Gough's example will be followed by other pupils or assistants in the neighbourhood.

" I fear however from what I have heard that the students are rather alarmed at what they call the ' stiffness ' of some of the questions and fearful of failure shrink from the thought of attempting before they know or have even tried their capabilities.

" It has occurred to me that we might as a Society of Architects and especially as belonging to and being part of an *Academy* of Fine Arts which up to the present time has done little or nothing of that work which is indicated by its title. I repeat that as representatives of Architecture in an *Academy* of Fine Arts we might well take upon ourselves the duty (so at least I hold it) of endeavouring to relieve anxious students from much of this unnecessary alarm by offering them the means of a preliminary Examination at our own rooms once a quarter.

" To a youth engaged as a pupil or assistant, having no means to test himself it must be unquestionably very discouraging to be turned back after the cost of time and money involved by a London Examination to say nothing of the home labour, lost—because undirected or of the feeling of being plucked which can only be fairly understood by the sufferers themselves.

" This year 9 only out of 17 passed the Examination. Had the unfortunate 8 essayed their powers in a local preliminary examination I think we should have had a more satisfactory result (in a general point of view) and I feel sure the students themselves would have been both happier and wiser.

" If you think my proposal good will you kindly move a resolution to further it in some way.

" I much regret that I am not able to take the active part I should wish in this subject as in the matters connected with the profession and our local Association, but I trust you will have no difficulty in impressing on the members of our Society the necessity of recognising the fact there are duties to be done as well as pleasures to be enjoyed by an associate body like ours, and that while they enjoy the latter in listening to the glowing descriptions and brilliant perorations which will no doubt enrich the lecture of this evening they will not forget that there is work to be done and duties to be fulfilled before we can be worthy of the alliance we enjoy with such active hard-working and influential Associations as those of Birmingham, Manchester, and Liverpool.

" Believe me

" My dear Mr. Gabriel

" Yours very sincerely

" EDWARD W. GODWIN."[1]

[1] The punctuation is as the original letter.

CHAPTER IV

LITTLE HOLLAND HOUSE

MEANTIME in London surprising events had occurred in the lives of the Terry sisters. Kate was now famous, Ellen married and retired from the stage. All this had happened within a year. For Kate this transformation had taken shape in the accepted dramatic manner. Her opportunity had come to her when the leading lady in *Friends and Foes* at the St. James's had, through illness, been unable to appear, and she, the understudy, had been called upon suddenly to play the part. She was just nineteen. A few observers had realised that she needed but such an accident to bring her genius to the notice of the public. Tom Taylor, the dramatic critic of *The Times*, was one of them.

Taylor was a man of considerable influence and kindly nature, small, dull and heavy in appearance, and careless in his dress. His spectacles were usually tied on with string in case they should be misplaced, for he was absent-minded. When he shook hands he hardly knew when to let go, seeming to be entirely unconscious of the passage of time. He was a friend of the girls' parents, a playwright, an art critic of sorts, and what was more to the point, he was really certain that in Kate Terry he had discovered an exceptional actress.

The morning following Kate's brilliant performance there appeared in *The Times* a eulogy that made all the town eager to flock to applaud her. She had become the talk of London. Taylor was delighted and felt rewarded as the report had been his own doing. She must have her portrait painted. His friend, G. F. Watts, was undoubtedly the most suitable artist, and, since he had persuaded many distinguished people to sit to him, it would not be difficult to persuade Watts to depict the tall and

45

beautiful young lady. The artist was quite agreeable to painting the picture if Taylor could make the arrangements for Kate Terry to pose.

The appointment for the sittings proved more awkward to arrange than Taylor had anticipated. Mrs. Terry insisted upon a chaperone. She herself had too much to do to be able to spare any of her time sitting about whilst any artist painted a portrait of her daughter. Ellen, the only other possible deputy, was young, and, moreover, as she helped her mother look after the rest of the children, could not be spared. She was performing in a tedious series of plays at the Haymarket, none of them in the least successful. She felt dissatisfied and ardently wished that something exciting would happen for her.

Tom Taylor, not to be denied, persisted, and at length managed to persuade her mother to allow Ellen to accompany her sister to the studio. Thus it befell that she tidied herself up and with Kate presented herself at Little Holland House, the home of Watts. There the artist, a delicate middle-aged man, lived, pampered by a trio of imposing women and the husband of one of them, his friend, Thoby Prinsep.

The ladies were sisters, Mrs. Prinsep, an energetic domineering woman of Bohemian ideas; Lady Somers, the beauty of the group; and Mrs. Cameron, a plain woman with a remarkable flair as a pioneer photographer. They were the daughters of James Pattle of the Bengal Civil Service. He had made a large fortune, but before he could retire to join his daughters in England he died in India. His widow, a French lady, had his remains preserved in a barrel with which she embarked for London. On the voyage home there had been trouble with the barrel and the remains of Mr. Pattle—" the greatest liar in history "—had been jettisoned into the ocean.

It was into this circle that Watts had been imported as a tame genius when ill, by Mrs. Prinsep, and established in the comparatively rural house on to which he had built a studio in which, when so disposed, he worked.

The three women were known to their friends as Beauty, Dash and Talent. If they needed any reinforcement they could summon the support of another four girls of the family. They had all the

THE SISTERS. (Kate and Ellen Terry).

A Bookcase.

possessive instincts strongly developed and Watts was their protégé, their property. His studio was haunted by celebrities who came to be painted by the artist ; or—swathed in hearthrugs and horse blankets—photographed by Mrs. Cameron.

The two young Terrys were far from the ordinary run of visitors to the house. They were so obviously dangerously beautiful and their background was that of touring actresses. Ellen, moreover, was charmed by the novelty of everything about the place and hypnotised by the deference paid to the painter. The visit was a new experience.

When Watts saw them both, he disregarded his instructions, and instead of painting a portrait of Kate alone, he decided to pose her with Ellen on one canvas as *The Sisters*. The thought was a considerate one as it was more flattering to Ellen to be depicted, than to be left in the background as an impatient spectator. There was more in the action than appeared. The hopeful Taylor and his wife, apparently unaware that she was engaged, had thought that perhaps Watts would fall in love with Kate ; instead, to their surprise, he was plainly more attracted towards her young sister. The impressionable artist had fallen in love, or thought he had, with Ellen. Singularly, Mrs. Prinsep, instead of being disturbed, encouraged the proposal. She did not allow Watts to lose any time, nor was Ellen given any chance to change her mind. If he could get the consent of her parents, there was no impediment to the marriage. He hadn't, like some suitors, to make his way in the world. In a worldly sense it was a good, a brilliant match.

Though she was hardly consulted, Ellen was not averse from the arrangement. She was fond of the artist in a daughterly fashion and was thrilled by the prospect of entertaining, as hostess, his visitors. She had always had a taste for the graces of cultivated society, and now the pleasant vista opened to her girlish eyes. Her brief encounter with Edward and his friends had stimulated her imagination. From now on she was to be the wife of a distinguished man, the hostess of his friends and the envy of the women who imagined they could have worn her shoes, with the depressing stage abandoned for ever. In anticipation the prospect was thrilling, it had the outline of a fairy story. Being a minor, mother and father must be induced to give their blessing, and under Mrs. Prinsep's impetuous blandishments, Mrs. and Mr. Terry gave their consent.

The engagement was very brief. Thus on January 20th, 1864, George Frederick Watts, aged forty-seven, and Ellen Terry, not yet seventeen, were married by the Reverend Dr. Fussey at the Church of St. Barnabas, Kensington. The bride was dressed in a golden-brown slashed silk dress, designed by the grave pre-Raphaelite friend of her husband, Holman Hunt. There were some amongst the friends present in the church who remarked that the marriage was a mistake.

The bride started to cry as they left the church and the middle-aged Watts consoled her by remarking—" It makes your nose swell."

This was the news of his friends which drifted down to Edward in Bristol, where he had just taken Henry Crisp as his partner. Kate Terry was undoubtedly entitled to all the applause she had gained—he had foretold her success in his own *Jottings*. Ellen, it seemed, had chosen a more secure, a more domestic career. He would call upon her when next he went to town by Brunel's railway. Thanks to Crisp it was possible to get up to London either on a visit to Burges or upon the business of the Alliance without leaving work unattended.

Still, his chief interest was in Bristol. The architects there had approved his suggestion to Mr. Gabriel that the junior members of the calling should have regional training facilities. In London there were the Academy schools and the British Museum. In Bristol there was nothing, or so it was said. Edward knew better. His pupil, Hannaford, had won a prize for a measured drawing of the chimney piece and roof in the Angel Inn, High Street. Because he knew better he was busy drafting a scheme for the education of the students in which the antiquities and more recent buildings in the vicinity were to play their part. All that was required was that someone should trouble to tell the youths what to measure.

At the moment he and Crisp were waiting hopefully for the result of the Congleton Town Hall Competition. It was made known in May, and he was again successful. This time he was

not so excited as he had been when the award for Northampton
was known. Nor were the architects of Bristol surprised. It
was the rest of England that felt the shock. It appeared to
Londoners that in future they would have to reckon with an
unknown from the provinces. Northampton might have been
a fluke, but now Congleton made the danger appear real. The
earlier Town Hall had been opened that month, when the day was
commemorated by the Mayor planting a tree, speeches by Lord
Lyveden, Lord Henley and others, followed by a dinner and
dancing in which Edward and his wife had joined.

About Congleton how did Godwin feel? " It was," he said,
" a small business. There was in the building a little influence of
French Gothic. *The Stones of Venice* had been dropped! "

When at length the Town Hall was completed, in his view its
only defect was the top of the tower. He used to say of it that if
and when he became a wealthy man he would rebuild that part
of the structure at his own expense. The building lacks variety
and is poorly sited.

Of course, Eastlake noticed the change in manner from that
in which Northampton had been designed.

" The general outline of the central tower and the open arcade
on the street level still indicate a lingering affection for southern
art ; but a French element predominates in the design, which
is simpler and more ascetic in character. This tendency to shun
the minutiae of decorative detail, to aim at effect by study of
masses of unbroken wall space, and by artistic proportion of
parts is perhaps the main secret of Mr. Godwin's artistic power."[1]

Congleton took two years to build. Most probably it was the
work that Godwin was to design between that time and the
publication of his book that prompted Eastlake to make his
final comment, for Congleton, though plain, is not distinguished
by " unbroken wall space ".

The competition system has the pernicious effect of inducing
the competitor to pander to the preference of the adjudicator
and so to assume a personality that is not his own. Although in
both these buildings Edward adopted the prevailing fashion,
and so won the competition (in the example of Northampton

[1] *A History of the Gothic Revival*, C. L. Eastlake, 1873, p. 358.

he had risked Tite's preference), he gave to their actual construction the individual stamp of his own mind. He was never
merely an imitator. Of his work Beresford Pite said, " his
buildings were designed with a view to the simplest and most
direct achievement of the purpose intended, and avoided architectural treatment as such ", confirming by this remark the trait
noticed by Charles Eastlake at a time when it was only to be
realised by comparison with buildings going up in the next
street.

He, Godwin, attained the artistic excellence of his stylistic
work through the refinement of his sense of perception. It
is noticeable that all his criticism of his own or other buildings
appeal to the sensation conveyed through the eye to the mind.
His constructional aptitude had been developed by his sojourn
with William Armstrong ; his utilitarian ideas implanted by his
father. His solutions were always right working ; and when he
fell short of his own aims he was never ashamed to point out the
errors into which he had fallen. The final arbitrament was the
mind's eye. His judgement was completely aesthetic.

Yet he had in his make-up gifts which were communicable.
In the month of July, Edward moved a step further on the road
he had indicated in his letter to Mr. Gabriel. He was not merely
a dreamer but an individual bubbling over with notions that led
to action. He proposed " that it is desirable to form a class to
be called the Students' Class, and that a committee be appointed
of three members to report on the course of study to be pursued".[1]
That was the other Godwin speaking, terse and practical. The
members of the Bristol Society of Architects readily agreed to
adopt his suggestion, the result being that a few weeks later a
programme, which bears the impress of his dominant part in its
composition, was placed before the members. The outline of
study to be followed was this :

(1) The History of Architecture and Subsidiary Arts.
(2) Drawing. In the Greek antique and the best work of the
     Middle Ages.
     From the Life. Anatomical lectures.

[1]Minutes : Bristol Architectural Society, July 4th, 1864.

Figure composition.
Modelling and Painting *in tempera.*
(3) Design. The science of construction and applied mathematics, including art processes.
(4) Languages.

In this programme his insistence on the relationship of the arts is noticeable. The prominence of drawing appears to be the combined proposal of Burges and Godwin. The former had in the debates at Conduit Street specially pressed the value of ability of this sort, and had complained that the programme proposed by the Institute did not call for anything of the kind. Godwin's programme shows an excess of drawing, especially of a non-architectural kind ; too little sanitation, ventilation, heating and the like. Still, the elements of building were very simple in the sixties and no doubt could be covered by the subject—The Science of Construction. As was indicated in his letter to the President, the scheme was designed to enable the youth of Bristol to try their hands at home before venturing to London to essay the R.I.B.A. Voluntary Examinations.

The Institute Examination had been approved in 1861, after prolonged discussion by the leading architects of the country. The programme was divided into two parts : (1) Ordinary Proficiency, (2) Honourable Distinction. With the exception of a language in the Distinction, the subjects were the same in either part, namely, Drawing and Design—a design for some building, or portion of a building, in the style named by the candidate, the subject being given by the examiners. Mathematics, Physics, Professional Practice, Materials, Construction, History and Literature completed the test. Out of a total of 6,000 marks, 1,750 were allotted to Drawing and Design ; 1,250 to History and Literature. The marks for the other subjects ranged between 500 to 750 a subject. In the Distinction, History and Literature were awarded the highest marks, 700.

At Bristol who was to act as instructor ? The students had hoped that Godwin would give his help. They wanted to have the advice of so redoubtable a designer, and were disappointed when they learned that this could hardly be. It was bruited that

he was intent upon moving to London, and indeed, nowadays he
was absent from Bristol on more days than he was present. The
work the firm had in hand was scattered between Worthing
and Portishead—at which place they were building a cottage.
Furthermore Godwin was—as the designer of the partnership—
constantly on the look-out for likely competitions, and if he
thought of entering was in the habit of visiting the site and staying
in the town before deciding whether to submit a design. Recently,
on this errand, he had spent some time at Retford and Chester,
where the councils proposed to build Town Halls from selected
competition drawings. The firm put in a design for Chester but
only secured a premium. Then the partners had undertaken to
complete the work of a Bristol architect, T. S. Hack. Mr. Hack
had died leaving a lot of work unfinished, and to help his widow
Godwin and Crisp had offered to complete the various buildings
and hand over to his widow the fees for these without deduction.
The largest of these undertakings were Stockland Church and
schools.

In Bristol he had some jobs for which he felt personally
responsible; a house for Mrs. Chettenham Guiness, and a
tombstone for the grave of the Rev. S. E. Day, the clergyman who
had baptised him. Although the memorial was very simple, a
lot of trouble was caused by the separate contractors for the
stonework and the iron railings failing to act in concert, and when
the parts met in the cemetery they did not fit. Edward was much
put out that just when he was anxious to serve his friends well,
this should happen. An admirer of Mr. Day had also engaged him
to design a tracery window with the glass for the east end of
St. Philip's Church. He was disappointed by the finished stonework, and the insertion of the leaded lights was deferred until
some time later.

Despite these many distractions and transactions, and the worry
due to the illness of his wife Sarah, who had recently become an
invalid, he drafted an important resolution which he proposed at
a meeting of the Bristol Society of Architects in November 1864:

" That a standing Committee be appointed to survey from
time to time the Ancient Architectural Monuments and remains

of Bristol and its neighbourhood in order to report to the Bristol Society of Architects thereon, with the view to promote the faithful conservation of such monuments and remains."[1]

The proposal, though local in its application as it was bound to be in the circumstances, was an anticipation by thirteen years of the similar suggestion of William Morris which originated the Society for the Preservation of Ancient Buildings.

The use, by Edward, of the word "conservation", not restoration, was prophetic.

Notwithstanding every care, life in the private rooms at 21 Portland Square was not progressing as happily as it was in the office. Mrs. Godwin's illness required quiet. She must not be disturbed by business callers ringing the bell. It was therefore unsuitable to have the office and the home in the same house, and the partners looked round for accommodation elsewhere. They found a suitable set of rooms at No. 2 Quay Street, and moved the furniture and drawings from Portland Square to the new address in March.

Ann Godwin, his sister, came to help look after the invalid and Edward at No. 21. The new arrangements gave Sarah and her husband some momentary relief.

The tenancy of Rupert Chambers (as the new offices were called) commenced on April 1st 1865. The firm rented four rooms and a cupboard on the second floor, with the proviso "a proper place for coal and of course use of a water closet in the house" stipulated for by the methodical Henry Crisp. The lower floors of the building were occupied by a wine merchant— an arrangement that suited Mr. Crisp's ideas of hospitality, for it saved him the trouble of writing letters ordering his whisky.

Unfortunately the removal proved to be of no benefit for the patient. Sarah Godwin's malady grew worse, and she had to be taken to 7 Apsley Place, Clifton—a home managed by a Mrs. Fowke. But it was of no avail, for Sarah Godwin died there in May. Her death was announced in the local press:

"May 3, at 7 Apsley Place, Clifton, Sarah, the beloved wife of Edward W. Godwin, Esq., architect."

[1]Minutes, November 2nd, 1864.

Very little is known about Sarah. She is said to have been beautiful, highly educated, cultured and artistic and much in love with her husband. Although so little is remembered of her person, there are several stories relating to her death which have come down the years. In brief these are that the brokers were in possession of the furniture at Portland Square; that when she lay dying upstairs Godwin was in a room on the ground floor and that he was summoned to her bedside by Crisp. When he entered the room his wife greeted him " Oh, Edward," and placed her arms about his neck. Godwin disengaged her hands and left the room. Yet another tradition is that before she died, she asked her husband to play on the organ a Bach fugue, to the strains of which she died.

It is difficult to reconcile these legends having regard to the particulars upon her death certificate. It is possible that they are each true, improbable that they happened at the same time. The organ was in Portland Square—the death was in Apsley Place. There may have been an organ or harmonium at Apsley Place, in which event he would have gone downstairs and played upon it; but because of the circumstances under which she died, the interview and her request must have taken place at the outset of her illness, some time before her removal. The organ playing may have occurred at Apsley Place, for unless it did, it could hardly have coincided with her death. It is most probable that these events—and it is difficult to believe that they were invented —have in course of time become confused in sequence.

What the brokers were doing is immaterial, for they figure like a chorus at the several crises of Godwin's life. If they were in fact in possession at the time in Portland Square, their presence must have been due to his preoccupation, for he was not then in any financial need.

Now that his wife was gone, the house was much too large for his requirements, and had unpleasant associations for him. There was little to hold him to Bristol. Crisp could well look after the work in the south-west from Rupert Chambers, having in fact done so for the past year, and should London prove inhospitable, Edward could return. Under the circumstances he could not be accused of deserting Bristol. The ladies of the City had decided to entrust to him the design of an elaborate reredos and sedelia to be built in the Church of St. Mary Redcliffe, but that and the partnership, and the Architectural Society, could be dealt with by journeys in the reverse direction—London to Bristol.

It was in October 1865 that he took the plunge and opened an office at 23 Baker Street, Portman Square, London. As soon as he was installed, he commenced the working drawings of Congleton Town Hall, and laboured very assiduously upon the preparation of three alternative designs for the Assize Courts proposed to be built in Bristol. Constant letters passed between the two partners. From Rupert Chambers, Crisp reported that he was negotiating the purchase of a site for the New Bristol Theatre Company, in the new street to be constructed from College Green : jointly Godwin and Crisp were making sketch designs for large industrial buildings for A. and J. Fry. This was not all, as they had four schools in hand for the Church of England : a memorial at Almondsbury and another at Oatlands for Lady Emily Gray, the last causing Godwin a lot of trouble owing to the slowness of the contractors who failed to complete on the day set apart for its dedication. They had promised over and over again that all would be ready, yet in the last week the ceremony had to be put off. Both in London and Bristol the partners were very much occupied. They were working on Saturday. One Saturday afternoon as Crisp was locking the door of the office a boy came hot-footed to him with a letter. Henry took the envelope from him and opened it standing on the pavement the while. Commencing to read . . .

" Oh! we've won the first prize! " he exclaimed.

" Read on! " prompted the excited bearer.

" Goodness me, we've won the second prize! "

" Read on! " persisted the youth.

" Good heavens, we've won the third! "

So it was that Henry Crisp learned the news that Godwin's designs had been awarded all the premiums, First, Second and Third in the Bristol Assize Court Competition, by the assessor Waterhouse. He telegraphed the news to Godwin in London. Edward was surprised, but the rest of the profession were astounded. It was, indeed, an extraordinary achievement.

The design by which he had won the first prize was one of the most successful of his compositions, yet in spite of its excellence, the authorities decided to hold a further competition for the same programme on another site. The Architectural Alliance protested but the Council persisted. Apart from the merit of his designs, one reason why he had gained all the awards was that he had observed a condition which stipulated that a strip of land, awkwardly intersecting the site, should be left free from building. This handicap had been no obstacle to Godwin ; neither the plan nor the elevation of any of his designs was in the least injured.

In an attempt to avert the rumoured intention of the promoters the partners wrote to the Town Clerk :

> " 23 Baker Street, London, and
> Rupert Chambers, Bristol.
> " July 5th 1866.

" DEAR SIR,

" We fear that the impression of some of the Town Council with reference to ourselves in connection with any future decision, as to the carrying out of either one of our designs for the Bristol Assize Courts, may be that having won the premiums we have gained the object of our labours in competing. Should this be at all the case, we would beg of you thro' this letter to remove any such impression, as our real desire in competing, was to look beyond any premium, and to succeed in obtaining the work and thereby secure to ourselves professional merit. At the same time we in no way undervalue the fact of our unlooked-for and entire success in thus being awarded the premiums. But we wish it to be distinctly understood that we had a higher aim in competing than competing for a premium ; our actual motive being the desire of ultimate success in being the architects of the building.

> " We are, Dear Sir,
> " Yours very obedly.,
> " GODWIN & CRISP.

" D. Burges Esq.,
" Town Clerk,
" Bristol."

As already said, the protest of the architects—the Alliance—and the press were of no avail, and the Council ordered another competition—for which, as Crisp afterwards exclaimed, " they foolishly entered ".

Edward was not unnaturally disappointed—" There were wheels within wheels," exclaimed Crisp when speaking of the resolution of the Council to hold another competition.

When later in the year Burges was invited to submit a design for the New Law Courts in London, he asked Godwin to collaborate in the large undertaking of the competition drawings. He agreed.

The two competitions were alike in nature, the problem in each was the same, the complexity and magnitude of the London building being the great difference. In order to save time by working together, Edward went to stay in Blackheath, at the home of Burges senior, a well-known engineer. True, the two architects wasted many hours in argument, all the while enjoying themselves hugely and producing eventually a design that embodied a lot of research, thought and draughtsmanship. They were unsuccessful, yet many critics were agreed with the opinion voiced later by M. B. Adams—" His design for the Law Courts was architecturally by far the best."[1]

As if all this activity were insufficient occupation, Edward frequented the British Museum where he read and examined all he could discover relating to Saxon building. His investigation of this period of architectural history was not unmixed with an interest in the life of Godwin, Earl of Wessex, for whom he had a lifelong curiosity.

Although he had these numerous undertakings in hand, perhaps because of them, he found sufficient leisure to attend the theatre. " Plays," he stated, " were restful." Indeed he advised architectural students to form the habit of playgoing twice a week, as was his own custom. Like Charles Dickens he was fond of walking ; every morning and evening it was his practice to go for a long walk, and he recommended the rule to others engaged in sedentary work.

Some of these walks ended at Little Holland House, where he

[1] *R.I.B.A. Journal*, July 27th, 1912, p. 643.

renewed his acquaintance with the juvenile Mrs. Watts and her husband, and joined in the light entertainment provided by Mrs. Prinsep for her collected guests. It did not take long for him to realise that life was not going as it should with the disparately matched husband and wife, nor to divine that Mrs. Prinsep and Ellen were at odds. Mrs. Watts was too active and tactless, and proper respect for the pompous Victorians was wanting in the lively young lady.

Watts' studio was festooned with studies of Ellen. She was evidently not only wife but patient model; Ellen as *Ophelia*; Ellen as *Choosing*: as *Watchman What of the Night*, showed the use to which she had been put. True they were his best paintings, done when he was in love. That was now ended. Her ineffectual husband treated her as a child. " Little girls must be seen and not heard " was the rule at Little Holland House. Instead of being acknowledged as the wife of Watts, Ellen found herself left to her own resources and naturally reacted by making her presence obvious when least wanted. It was Mrs. Prinsep who did the entertaining, presiding at the tea tables under the elms, while afterward the guests played bowls or croquet on the lawn. In a sense Watts and his wife were but lodgers in the Prinsep's household. The serious dreamy George Frederick had become more than usually easily fatigued, having made the discovery that his spirited wife was very tiring. She was too young, not sufficiently awed by his acquaintances. The place was full of celebrities whose portraits by Watts crowd the walls of the National Portrait Gallery. Ellen was only there to be corrected and restrained—the three women saw to that. Watts was too deeply in their debt to venture to make any defensive protest, and even if Ellen had been older, she and he would have had to be sufficiently resolute to cut themselves adrift from the Prinseps.

The arrival of Edward came as a relief to her; here was someone who treated her as possessed of intelligence; someone who knew all about the stage, its habitués, the plays of Shakespeare, Bristol, her parents and her childhood days—so near and yet so distant. Every one of these memories provided the two with a theme for endless conversational variations. Edward was understanding, he saw through the whole façade of pretence. All women found him fascinating and Ellen was not excepted. Unlike most men he had a flair for women's dress, was appreciative of colour, form and arrangement about them. Other men ignored their costumes and were unconscious of their setting. Godwin specialised in costume and was sensitive to line, and the motion of the body was for him more revealing than spoken words. For his part he admired Ellen, felt her presence stimulating, and thought that Watts was neglectful.

The artist was now forty-eight, Edward thirty-two, while Mrs. Watts was but a young seventeen, as always, lovely to look upon, careless and bewitchingly graceful. They were neighbours. They became close friends. When free from Mrs. Prinsep they were different people. Ellen had a real affection and respect for her husband. Godwin also had much in common to debate with the artist who was the foremost of those artists in between the academic and non-academic painters, Thomas Armstrong and Albert Moore.

On occasion Ellen and her husband visited Edward and he them. Mrs. Watts when out alone frequently looked in to see him and nobody thought anything ill of her doing so. It was in this casual manner that, calling upon him one evening, she found him to her surprise, unwell and in bed unattended. Ellen was much upset by her discovery and set about making poultices for him. " You see, I was a very kind little girl."[1]

Innocently heedless of the conventions (that was one of the faults unconventional Mrs. Prinsep tried to remedy), or of any misconstruction that might be placed upon her actions, she stayed to look after him. Much to her concern when she got home she found her parents and husband in " solemn conclave ". They accused her of infidelity and professed themselves horrified by what she had done. Protesting her innocence, she tried to defend her action, but it was all to no effect. In the true spirit of melodrama her indignant parents turned her adrift. Her husband vowed he would never speak to her again, and overlooked the way he had himself entered Little Holland House. It is charitable

[1]*Discretions and Indiscretions*, Lady Duff Gordon, 1932.

to conclude that he had been pushed into asserting himself by the sisters whose protégé he was. Distraught, she appealed to other members of her family, but they declined to listen to the story. Godwin either would not or could not intervene. There was nothing to do but leave Little Holland House, her illusions shattered.

Chapter V

AN IRISH CASTLE

THE LITTLE HOLLAND HOUSE group tried to explain the breach as due to incompatibility, which was in part true. For her part, Mrs. Terry relented sufficiently to admit Nelly to her home and provide a room for her. There she sat disconsolate, hoping against hope that her husband would come and claim her. But it was not to be. The Prinseps did not wish any reconciliation, and there being no other solution agreeable to Ellen, she reluctantly returned to the stage.

Godwin, the unwilling excuse for the break-up, had no deep regrets. He was quite ready to go through with the whole business and marry Mrs. Watts if her husband saw fit to divorce her. Ellen, however, was in no such mood—she was not in love—and felt that the experience had been unreal. On the other hand, Edward believed that in time the situation would develop in his favour. In his view Watts was tired of his wife and the incident had been used as an excuse to get rid of a trying partner. If he could go so far as to separate on such trivial grounds, might he not eventually go further? At length, in order to try to regularise the situation, the Little Holland House people contrived to draw up a legal separation which, like the marriage, was arranged. Outsiders had more to say in the contract than the parties concerned.

In London, Godwin was still the representative of the Bristol Architects. The Society had recently decided to extend its influence by electing laymen as members, and one of these, the Earl of Limerick, was made President. With him Godwin was elected Vice-President, for he continued to go down to Bristol at intervals and to have business and social attachments there. Indeed he took the chair when the President was absent, and entered into the Society's discussions with his old enthusiasm. The award in the second Assize Court Competition had just been made: Pope—" a wretched mean fellow "—and Bindon 1st Premium; Godwin and Crisp 2nd. Godwin's design, while better than the winners, was an over-ornate building. It was not unlike that which had pleased in Northampton, for he had been told by someone that the city council wanted an elaborate elevation.

Why Godwin and Crisp were passed over has never been explained. Neither the profession nor the press could understand. Both partners were at a loss. " Wheels within wheels," said Crisp. " Gerrymandering," thought Godwin. They were not unpopular, nor could anything be said against either as to characters as men, or their qualifications as architects. He had now been elected a Fellow of the Society of Antiquaries, in which capacity he had just published two pamphlets on archaeological themes, one on *St. Alban's Abbey*, the other on *Ancient Bristol*. That on *Ancient Bristol*, with another on *The Foundation of St. Mary and St. Mark*, was based on matters about which he had talked to the Architectural Society in the past. It was considered that they were a sufficiently valuable contribution to local history to be read, in his absence, at the Bristol meeting of the Somerset Archaeological Society. The reason why he was not present at any of the meetings was because he was, at the time (August 1867), in Ireland with Burges and the Earl of Limerick, his latest client.

The Earl, who had been persuaded by his sister, Lady Gray, to engage Edward, was a learned and congenial man who had been impressed by Godwin's attainments and personality, when they had met as officers of the Architectural Society. He was a Chaucer enthusiast who had soon discovered that Edward knew all about the Pilgrims who went from the Tabard Inn in Southwark to the shrine of St. Thomas. Moreover Edward had shown himself to be a most capable architect. It was Limerick's desire that Edward should design for him a castle at Dromore near Pallaskenny in Ireland. So in August, with Burges, who had still work on hand in Ireland, Edward went to inspect the possibilities of the Limerick estate as providing an appropriate site for the castle.

On the way there, he and Burges stayed at a remote hotel for the night. Next morning, after a long discussion the previous evening, Edward, on coming down to breakfast, found that Burges " had sketched on the margin of a newspaper two thirteenth-century architects in a most comical encounter with the legend ' *Willar de Honecourt et Petrius de Corbie inter le disputantes* ' ".[1] This was doubtless a revised version of the similar drawing in the architect de Honecourt's sketch-book —the kind of action that Burges was famed for. Arrived at Pallaskenny, Edward stayed with the Earl, and together one autumn morning they chose the position of the castle-to-be. It was a dreamlike situation " on the edge of a wood, overlooking a lake, which reflected the castle, one hundred feet below ".[2] In the distance the River Shannon could be glimpsed.

Before he started any work on the drawings of the building, he visited and measured a dozen or more castles, now in ruins, in the country. It is almost certain that Burges was with him the whole time. When he had made these studies, and thought he knew something about the construction of Irish mediaeval castles, he made the design. The walls of the new Dromore were from three to six feet thick. The principal apartment in the castle, the banqueting hall, was to be fifty-six feet long, thirty feet wide and thirty-six feet high. The gateway, twenty-three by thirty by sixty feet high.[3]

As the site was too far from London to admit of the architect inspecting the work as often as he should, a resident clerk of works was employed to supervise the construction. The con-tractor was an Englishman. For two years the work of building continued. Eastlake pronounced the finished building " a most successful work ". The architect though, as will appear, not unaware of some mistakes, was charmed by the result of his labours, it was as if a dream had been realised. " He had seen it by moonlight, seen it from the road, at a distance from every angle, and the silhouette was about as charming a thing as ever he saw in his life."

While some are inclined to believe that self-praise is unreliable, when Edward bestowed it there is reason to take notice. He was

[1] *The Art Journal*, 1886, p. 170.
[2] *The British Architect*, November 29th, 1878.
[3] Illustration in *The Building News*, November 1st, 1867.

D

far too prone to condemn all his own work and to dwell upon the defects than to speak of the merits. He applied the same critical standard to himself as to his judgement of others, and this clearsighted acknowledgement of mistakes was a means of registering the memory of them and so avoiding their repetition. He never attempted to excuse his faults.

The interior of the castle was considered as carefully as had been the exterior. The walls of the principal apartments had been decorated by H. Marks, A.R.A., with figures in outline, filled in with plain, unshaded colours. Over the mantelpiece a peacock provided the theme of decoration in anticipation of things to come.

The Earl was delighted at the realisation of his ambition, notwithstanding that the castle had one amusing and one serious defect. The first consisted in that the gateway to the court exactly suited the time of Edward the First, was not adapted to the days of Queen Victoria, when a four-in-hand with passengers on top had an uncomfortable time trying to gain an entry. They preferred to arrive on foot.

The serious trouble was due to damp. Although the walls were six feet thick and waterproofed, the damp penetrated them, and the decorations by Marks were spoiled. These decorations had been contracted for at forty shillings a square foot, the then prevalent system. Edward thought it was a stupid custom, and decided never to employ an artist on such terms again. Artists cannot be expected to work to measure.

As had been the case at Northampton, he designed all the furniture and furnishings. When the castle was completed, Edward came to the conclusion that Ireland was not the place for an Englishman to practise; the climate was too humid, and to cope with it properly required special knowledge. Nor are the difficulties of Irish west-coast conditions generally realised.

While Edward was flitting about between England and Ireland, he used his partner's home as his point of departure for Limerick and Glenbegh, where the partners were building a large house for the Hon. Roland Winn. When in London he spent some time with Ellen. Why not, he persisted, end the ridiculous situation— give Watts the grounds for divorce and bring the issue to a

NORTH·WEST·ASPECT·OF·DROMORE·CASTLE·C͞O·LIMERICK·THE·PROPOSED·RESIDENCE·OF·THE·EARL·OF·LIMERICK

GODWIN & CRISP, ARCHITECTS.

climax ? For his part and hers, they might as well go through
with their episode, rather than continue to be regarded askance,
for he was in love, perhaps had been in love since he had helped
to make Titania's dress.

Though Ellen had perforce returned to the stage, she was very
unsettled. Unable to come to any decision, or to put any enthusiasm into her acting, she felt aggrieved that she had been
badly treated by her husband and her family. Undoubtedly she
had been ; if she had not been so young, if Watts had been more
of a man and less of a mollycoddle, things would never have
fallen out as they had. A few of her elderly friends did what little
they could to console her. Tom Taylor, in a remote degree the
cause of the imbroglio, said that the whole affair was a tragic
mistake, but even so, he could do no more than be sympathetic.
He was sure that Watts had used the incident as a pretext to get
rid of his juvenile wife. In his middle-aged way he advised her
to cultivate her art—Charles Reade or he could write her parts.
Cultivate her art; that was the very thing she could not concentrate upon.

Young and beautiful, suffering under a sense of frustration, unable to explain her situation without involving others, she did not
know what to do. Unwanted by her husband and tied to him
by the artificial deed of separation, she was denied her freedom
and whispered about by gossips who knew only that something was wrong and imagined the rest. Small wonder that
she was unhappy and that she was making no progress in
her profession.

In October an incident occurred that seemed to confirm her
feelings. She was acting the part of Rose de Beaurepaire, the
sister of the heroine Josephine in *The Double Marriage*. The
play was one of the many by the tall, ungainly, happy-go-lucky
Charles Reade, Fellow of Merton, and sometime collaborator
with Tom Taylor. In this play, Mrs. Watts had to take a child
in her arms and declare it her own. " To her well-grounded skill
was entrusted this striking incident ", noted the author in
his journal. He was boyishly enthusiastic about his own plays,
and if they failed, it was never through any weakness in the
play, but always that of the actors or the audience.

On the first night when Ellen took the child and exclaimed, " I am its mother ", the audience hooted the play off the stage. So said Reade. The victim told the story in a more amusing way. "He had a line 'Whose child is this?' and there was I looking a mere child myself, and with a bad cold in the head too, answering, 'It's bine!'" Without doubt the last version is the best, and more likely to be accurate. The engagement in *The Double Marriage* was followed by a part in *Still Waters Run Deep*, an early play by Tom Taylor in which sex was fully discussed, and then as Kitty in *The Household Fairy*.

It was now the spring of 1868 ; almost three years had passed since her parting from Watts. He was not comfortable about the situation, and her conscience seems to have troubled Mrs. Prinsep. They were discussing overtures for a reunion, but it was too late.

During the run of this prophetically named play, *The Household Fairy* at the Queen's Theatre, Long Acre, Ellen made up her mind—and telling no one of her decision, she left the stage.

None of her friends knew where she had gone, or what had happened to her. She had disappeared completely. Her parents feared the worst because the one thing they knew for certain was that she was suffering under a sense of grievance. When the police fished out of the Thames the body of a fair, tall, slender young woman, Mr. Terry was asked to go to the mortuary to identify the corpse as that of his daughter. This done, the younger children were put into mourning. Ellen was no more. Then, suddenly, Mrs. Terry remembered that her daughter had a birthmark on her left arm, and hastened to confirm or happily disprove her husband's fateful identification. The body bore no such scar! In a measure, this discovery was a relief, yet it did not solve the mystery, nor had Ellen been found.

In fact, Ellen had no such birthmark on her arm, so her mother's discovery proved nothing. Yet it proved everything to her parents ; it gave them confidence that she might yet be found.

CHAPTER VI

A COUNTRY COTTAGE

SAFE IN a cottage facing Gustard Wood Common, Ellen and Edward were completely unconscious of these alarms. Possibly Tom Taylor had a suspicion as to what had happened. Charles Reade professed complete ignorance. The two culprits had barely settled down in their retreat when one morning Ellen overheard someone mention her name to another, explaining to the friend that she had been " found dead—drowned ". This startling rumour was too much for her peace of mind, and she could not rest until she had gone up to London to show herself alive and well to her distracted family. That, at least, was some consolation and relief for them, though all their persuasions could not induce her to return to the stage. The possibility of any reconciliation with Watts was gone.

She was now twenty-one, her own mistress, and the trials of the last three years had matured her. The pleading of her lover had at length touched her heart. Come what may, she would risk everything to make a success of the adventure she had embarked upon, and show herself in real life the Household Fairy.

Godwin was thirty-five, an age when it is said that man has reached maturity, settled ways, and given proof of the range of his ability. He could look back upon a career that had been on the whole successful. No one could say that he had wasted his opportunities. .Indeed he had made all those that he had had ; all he had accomplished was due to his own exertions, no influential connections had paved the way for him. Self-reliant, he had made his own position. Luck had played no part in his life.

In appearance he was of middle height, an elegant, slender, distinguished man who stood out in any company. His conversational powers were marked. He knew as much of Shakespeare, Chaucer and Spenser as any scholar, and his memory of the words of the authors he favoured enabled him to quote them on the instant. He was a very studious man.

The young men of his time regarded him as the greatest living designer. Some of the seniors, his contemporaries, complained that he had an ill-concealed contempt for their pretensions. His opinions were classed as trenchant—the polite way of intimating that they were outspoken. Indeed he never minced words upon any subject about which he felt deeply. Nor was he unconscious of his habit—he confessed as much, with Burges as victim. Upon those men who did not know him completely his brusque manner and emphatic intonation had an unfortunate effect, they do not appear to have made any allowance for the emphasis of debate or conversational argument. Now that he had flouted the conventions, he tended to wear arrogance as a protective cloak. For the same reason his action gave the self-satisfied, when they learned the news, something tangible to moralise about.

His friends Burges, J. P. Seddon, the architect who befriended Rossetti, and Phené Spiers were of a less conventional turn of mind, they knew the real man and understood him. Burges was ready to help, for of all men he knew more of the facts than any, and with that familiarity, and his own reputation, was equipped for contest with any traducers. Seddon thought Edward had been rash, yet hoped for the best. Spiers was content to consider him as an artist of genius—with the associated frailties.

As for Edward and Ellen, they had eloped, were happy and in love, blind and careless of the consequence. Gustard Wood— a mile from Wheathampstead, which was the place to which they had retired—was secluded, sleepy and idyllic. Fortunately Ellen had been trained by her mother to perform all the domestic duties. She had been the little mother to her brothers and sisters, and knew all about housekeeping under difficulties, for of those inconveniences she had had years of experience in theatrical lodgings. Now, alone with Edward, she commenced to recover her spirits and enjoy the adventure of life in the country. Still it was not all roses.

The day commenced when she rose at six o'clock and fed the livestock—they kept some hundreds of ducks and hens and a goat. Then she lit the fires, prepared the breakfast, and after attending to the pony which drew the trap in which she drove Edward to the station, she returned to scrub the floors, wash up and work in the garden.

The morning milk was delivered by a small boy called Fred Archer. Fred was just Fred and no one of his customers could foresee the renown that was later to be his. In the evening, Ellen walked across the common swinging a can to fetch the milk from the farm ; so far as anyone in Mackery End knew or cared, she was merely ' Nelly '.

Edward commenced his day at six o'clock, he had done so since his boyhood and was to do so until the end. He went to town by train when necessary—though he did as much as possible of his drawing at home in the cottage. He worked there on the details for Dromore Castle, which included the leaded lights, painted decoration of the walls and the furniture. In addition, he began the drawings for another large house, or fortress, in that dangerous practice ground—Ireland.

This establishment was for the Hon. Roland Winn at Glenbegh, County Kerry. It was almost as big as Congleton Town Hall. The plan was a hundred and thirty feet long and eighty-five feet wide. As usual with him, he added a tower more than a hundred feet high. Like Dromore it was modelled on the mediaeval precedents every self-respecting Irish client still required of his architect. It had in fact been commissioned at the same time (in 1867) as Dromore.

Nor had Northampton passed entirely unnoticed. The Marquis of Northampton admired it and, joining the Mayor as a patron, appointed Godwin to restore Castle Ashby and to build the gate lodges.

Work at Glenbegh Towers was started in March 1868. At the same time as the house, a small post office was built near the forked road, the whole undertaking was supervised by the Clerk of Works, Solomon Turner of Bristol, who, armed with piles of drawings by Godwin, and plied with copious letters from Crisp, did his best to comply with the Code of Rules given him for guidance by the Architects.

The labour was recruited locally by the agent Shea for the owner, the Hon. Roland Winn. The nonconformist Crisp advised Mr. Turner in his first letter " to beware of the priests ". The materials, chiefly from the neighbourhood, were paid for by the agent, the labour by the Clerk of Works, who forwarded the accounts to Rupert Chambers. The shell of the building was composed of stone walling two feet six inches thick, a cavity and an inner brick lining. The client was very difficult, Crisp exceedingly careful, the Clerk of Works anxious to please everyone. In the end the cost exceeded the estimate! And, notwithstanding every precaution, the autumn gales from the Atlantic drove the rain through the walls, or so it was thought, down which it poured—on the inside. Crisp went to Glenbegh to see for himself. On his return he wrote to three or four firms who owned the secret of proprietary brands of damp-resisting solutions. The reason for the excess of cost was due to a combination of factors. The first estimate was too low, the labour was slow, sometimes due to temperament of the Irish labour, sometimes because the materials ordered by the agent, Shea, had not reached the site when they were needed. Nor was the client free from blame, he added the tower and a circular room as an afterthought. The wet was a mystery. Edward had this news by post from his partner.

If Ellen was overworked, Edward was by no means idle. His work, while still that of the revival, was based on the study of the vernacular of the neighbourhood in which it was sited. It had its place. Their romance did not appear to have frightened away the clients, they were actually more in number and importance than before, and it quickly disclosed his friends.

When they had settled themselves at Gustard Wood or Mackery End, Burges came down to stay with the pair. He was not the man to desert his companions of Portland Square. They had so many interests in common and were so different in temperament, that they found each other's society invigorating. Although Edward was not devoid of humour it was of a dry kind.

That of his friend was more robust and sometimes unintended. The robust sort led him to suggest that the architectural prizes should be " shot for ", this due to his recruitment to repel the Crimean invasion. His unconscious humour when he specified " a cracked step ", or when, being in a bad temper, he condemned the workmanship that a few weeks later he praised. Ellen liked William Burges and enjoyed his cheerful presence.

Burges' principal employment at the time was the design for the tower to Cardiff Castle and interior decoration of the same for the Marquis of Bute. For this a great number of drawings were needed to give " scope for the designer's luxuriant fancy ". Ellen was induced to help him. With her own hands she made tracings of the whole of the decoration of the rooms in the Tower.

Everything seemed to promise well for the lovers. Together they planned to build a house at Harpenden into which they could move when it was finished. In anticipation of the day, Ellen set out and planted the garden in which it was to stand. Edward sketched his designs for the furniture, and in the lamplight, of an evening, made pencil drawings of his beautiful companion. They read and talked about Shakespeare's plays. On those days when he went up to London by train, Ellen harnessed the pony and drove to the station.

On January 18th, 1871, the partnership with Crisp came to an end.

A week before it was terminated, Edward received, from his partner in Bristol, a letter which told him that Crisp had heard from the contractor for Dromore that he was going to bring an action against the Earl of Limerick. As Godwin would no doubt be called as the principal witness, Crisp enquired if there was anything that the other side could take hold of to discredit his testimony ?

Edward replied by the next post from Albany Street admitting that he had sold some designs for furniture to the contractor.

Ten days later a further letter arrived from Bristol : in this Crisp said he had heard that the contractor had paid him £600, " Is this correct ? " To this Godwin replied that he had sold the " royalty " of some furniture designs; whether he mentioned the amount received or not, he apparently did not dispute with, or correct Crisp.

A little more than a fortnight elapsed when a further letter came from Crisp, stating that he had heard that Godwin had told the contractor to add £600 to the contract, and that he had " demanded and recovered " the money. " Does Lord Limerick know ? " To this serious charge Edward replied that Crisp was repeating " hearsay remarks ".

Two days later Crisp wrote repeating the charge in detail, and threatening to inform the Earl. To this letter Edward made no reply and so, still not satisfied, Crisp wrote to Lord Limerick enclosing copies of the correspondence. It does not appear to have been thought strange by Crisp that the transaction should be mentioned by the contractor to him when the final amounts were being considered. Since Crisp's letters are all the evidence available, and what Godwin said in reply can only be gathered from such fragments as are quoted by Crisp in the correspondence and the tenor of Crisp's own letters, we have not the entire story. It is curious that Crisp should have written the first of these letters if all that he had been told before writing was that a lawsuit against the Earl was imminent. It appears as if he had been told, at the time, the full story, but that he refrained from repeating what he had been told. When, however, his partner replied that he had sold furniture designs, the interval that took place between the receipt of this letter and his reply suggests that he had been in consultation with the contractor, who either repeated his statement or amplified the partial statement he had already made. As reported by Crisp, these charges were very definite and very serious. It is noticeable that Godwin replied very promptly to all but the last letter, and that he ignored. For the moment the matter dropped.

Following the dissolution of the partnership, his London office was still at 197 Albany Street. From there he had made his periodic visits to Dromore and his rare journeys to Glenbegh, which had been left in Crisp's hands to supervise. His experience in the design of municipal buildings was recognised by his appointment as consulting architect for Plymouth Town Hall by Hine and Norman ; indeed, some knowledgeable persons suggested that he was in fact the designer, and there is hardly room for doubt that he had a good deal to do with the design, for he had helped the architects with their drawings. Mr. W. A. Pite's copy of the illustration is endorsed " E. W. Godwin, F.S.A., responsible for design ". In fact he was paid for it by the architects. Of course, these employments necessitated his leaving Ellen alone at home. In London he had evening engagements at the meetings of the Architectural Association, in which he took a lively part. At Conduit Street, the Royal Institute of British Architects had at long last persuaded him to allow them to elect him a Fellow, and they had also made him a member of the Council which met in the small front room of James Wyatt's Greek house, their headquarters. Sir William Tite was the President and possibly it was he who had convinced Edward that he could be of help to the profession by becoming a member. In London also he was appointed one of the committee to advise on the situation of the railings at the west end of St. Paul's. The meetings of the Archaeological Association claimed his attendance at Weymouth and elsewhere. All these and many more appointments that it would be tedious to recite took him away from home from time to time. If he had lived in London, conditions would hardly have been any different.

For Ellen, left alone at Mackery End, these absences were very trying. She was lonely, and was always anxiously waiting for his return. When for some reason he had been detained, or overstayed his appointed time, she, so full of anticipation, had driven the little pony-cart in the dark to the dim-lit station, had perforce to return, depressed, alone to the house. She let her vivid imagination run wild and could not sleep, but turned over in her mind all the possible reasons for his absence. Had he deserted her ? Who was he with ? Was an accident the cause ? The scratching of mice in the still night frightened her unduly. . . . Someone told her to sleep in the open air, and, taking the advice, she lay all night watching the silver moon sail over Gustard Wood Common until she could keep her eyes open no longer, but slept. To make the situation more trying a baby girl had been born for whose future she was anxious. To help her with the child she had taken a companion, the doctor's wife, Mrs. Rumball, or " Boo " as she was afterward nicknamed, who came to live with her. Watts was still unforgiving ; even the advent of the child had not influenced him.

But when Edward reached home everything was changed and the sun shone. She could laugh at herself when she forgot to remove the giblets from the bird and served it at dinner whole. Together they read each one of Shakespeare's plays and then set down in writing their views of the presentation. Actually he was more at home than is usual with a professional man.

As we know already, Godwin held decided views on matters of taste which he did not hesitate to express freely in public ; in private he was even more dogmatic and sometimes violent. In his own house he could not bear the sight of an object which he thought harmful. As Mr. Rose declared, he was one of those " distinguished artists who, resolving to make their whole lives consistently perfect, will, on principle, never admit a newspaper into their houses that is of later date than the times of Addison ".[1] He believed that things seen affected the mind, particularly of those who were young. Clothes of too rigid a shape, that constrained the figure of the wearer, or of colours that were too blatant or discordant, must be forbidden. Books with seemingly innocent illustrations that did not satisfy his idea of line were not to be allowed. Toys had to be made of wood. Of course he never brought such objects into the house. Thoughtless but well-intentioned friends and relatives were the unwitting bearers of these unwelcome gifts. When found they had to be destroyed and he destroyed them. His little girl must be spared the corruption of her taste at all costs. The books he favoured were those which had illustrations by Walter Crane. In order that she should grow up with impeccable perception he chose her books, designed her and her mother's clothes. The dresses were kimono fashion, or of a Grecian character. He, Ellen and the child went hatless ; a habit deemed queer by the natives who were not accustomed to their middle-class neighbours behaving like themselves. In the 1870's to be conspicuous was a social affront and needed courage.

[1] W. H. Mallock, *The New Republic*. Mr. Rose concealed Walter Pater.

Of none of these actions did Ellen ever complain ; she had her own faults, carelessness, untidiness, natural indifference to money values—if such are faults. Moreover, men were the masters in Victorian England. In the eyes of outsiders his conduct was thought to be extraordinary and by common standards it was, but he was not a common man. He was a man of genius, who, like all such, knew his condition and realised his superiority. Few can understand that colour or form should excite anyone sufficiently to provoke such behaviour. As unsightly objects are far from rare, objectors are not unknown, though usually the objects destroyed are the property of the destroyer. In this case they were gifts to his daughter whom he was bent on preserving from the effect of ugly surroundings. He had not forgotten the part that Earl's Mead had played in his own life.

This destruction of things is a form of relief for those who feel that their own standards are not appreciated ; it is an aspect of the feeling, " the Lord thy God is a jealous God, Thou shalt have no other gods but me " ; a means of retaliation against the unseen forces that obstruct the ego. Beauty and ugliness are impossible to define—save possibly as fitness. Godwin found beauty in the ivories and pottery of the East which some of his friends thought unbearable. Whenever Edward was at home, life could not be dull—although he had some of the oddities of the Rev. Patrick Brontë.

In their respective spheres Edward and Ellen were both artists ; Edward recognised and excused by the perceptive, Ellen as yet undiscovered but subconsciously aware of her potentialities. They were neither of them easy to live with. Self-willed as they both were, they quarrelled and made it up as lovers will.

In 1871 Godwin entered for another Town Hall Competition. His other two town halls were finished, and now with the advent of a child his responsibility had increased. This time the building was for Leicester. George Edmund Street, R.A., was the assessor of the forty sets of plans submitted to him. The verdict was, " In my opinion there is no other design equal to it"—and so saying he awarded the first premium to Edward Godwin, F.S.A., F.R.I.B.A.[1] The design which won Street's approval is probably

[1] Illustrated in *The Architect*, January 6th, 1872.

the finest of all Godwin's buildings in the Gothic manner. It was larger than Northampton and had a small part of the elevation treated in a similar manner, namely the figures on pedestals, under canopies, ranged along the front—a favourite motif of his. The upper stories are set back so correcting the fault he had discerned in Northampton. The Clock Tower is much more powerful than any of his other towers. Unfortunately for him the Corporation decided to hold another contest, and on this account Godwin's *tour-de-force* was never built. The amount of labour in the drawings for this competition was immense. A month later the result of yet another competition, that for Winchester Town Hall, was made known. In this, Godwin's design was placed second. This was a new experience ; worse still, to rub salt in the sore, the winner had re-used the plan of Northampton Town Hall, though the site was an island and not, as had been Northampton, hemmed in on each side by buildings. When the winning design and that by Edward had been published, the critics and the correspondents in the building press voiced their disappointment that such a decision should have been made, for the second was so plainly the better design. The occasion was used by the complainants to draw attention to the dreadful appearance of the New Bristol Assize Courts built from the design of Pope, that had been substituted for the winning plans of Edward in the first abortive contest. It was stated emphatically that Godwin had twice been robbed of his rightful reward. The victim took the blows philosophically, saying nothing until several years later, though naturally these happenings must have been an acute disappointment.

Up to this time the most advanced mind in the profession had been obliged to ring the changes on the many varieties of Gothic. The designs for Chester, Winchester and Leicester had each been in the mediaeval manner. Ever since 1850 there had been complaints that the style was non-representative of the nineteenth century. However, no real alternative had appeared to gain approval. The classical devotees had built well into the half-century, and the Italian renaissance, fenestrated to admit more light in North Europe, had been exploited in the cities of Bradford, Manchester and Newcastle for the accommodation of industry. The Gothic in self-defence had tried to combine plate glass and cast-iron. The example of the Crystal Palace had been disparaged as engineering. Thomas Harris had written a pamphlet lauding the Hyde Park miracle but had failed to interest any patron. Godwin had said openly : " The day of architectural revivals may be setting—I for one sincerely hope it is."[1]

Edward, unlike Scott, Street, or Burges, who used their pens in defence of the pointed arch, never committed himself in print to any opinion in the battle of styles. He was content to be master in the use of neo-Gothic for as long as buildings of that order were preferred. His youth had been spent in accumulating the necessary historical and technical knowledge ; his early manhood had seen the use to which his labour could be put. All his designs have a unique personal touch save the Church of St. Johnston. They relied, as Eastlake had discovered, on simplicity—a frequent use of blank wall space and a dramatic arrangement of voids and ornament, when the programme admitted of such treatment.

The private commissions that he was engaged upon at this time were all such as required a knowledge of Gothic methods —Little Gaddesden Church and St. Philip, Stepney. The first of these was criticised by an anonymous correspondent in the *Building News* as phallic in conception.

When he was able to please himself, his designs had a Japanese character—though Godwin attributed the same characteristics to Celtic influences. For the ten previous years, his private surrounds had shown a preference for oriental lines. He had, from 1860 onward, devoted as much time to the study of Japanese art and its principals as, in the previous ten, he had employed upon mediaeval research. As yet only a few intimates were aware of this, although the illustrations of the Dromore interiors had revealed the fact to the discerning.

The secret of his success as a designer exercised those men who thought about theory. At the Institute they debated it, concluding eventually that it lay in the placing of Gothic features in a Grecian or classic frame. That was the opinion of R. P. Spiers and Professor R. Kerr, arrived at after a study of his executed works. They appear to have disregarded the plan as a source of propriety.

Change was in the air. In 1870 the Education Act had become law, and the London School Board, to meet its requirements, was obliged to erect a great many schools. To do this at a reasonable cost and to admit adequate daylight, it was imperative to find a less complex form of building than pseudo-Gothic in which to house the children. The architects engaged to design the schools selected the red-brick architecture of the reign of Queen Anne and the early Georges as their model. A step in this direction had always appeared probable, for it was at this point, it was felt, that architecture had ceased to evolve.

There had recently been premonitory signs. For example, Godwin, who was much involved in the management of the affairs of the Architectural Association, had given a prize for the students of design. The subject that he set for the contest was the plans and elevation of a London house with a frontage to the street of twenty-four feet. He had awarded the prize to H. A. Avern for a design in the Queen Anne manner. Despite his changing views, he took part in the discussions upon the Law Courts, contributing, generously, an article in defence of G. E. Street. He had recently resigned his membership of the Institute, having always been critical of the leadership of the profession—or art, as he insisted it be considered.

At this period a series of articles was appearing under Godwin's signature upon " Modern Architects and their Work ". T. H. Wyatt was discussed as an exemplar of the Palladians ; David Brandon of the Elizabethans ; Professor Kerr of the Academy Gothic ; Sir G. G. Scott (now knighted) of the Country Gothic. None of them found any favour in his eyes, but they were excused by him, since " we are the slaves of those who will employ us and not their leaders ".[1]

His articles provoked great interest, and one correspondent wondered aloud :

" We hardly know whether E. W. G. is centuries before or centuries behind his time. Had he lived in, and participated in rearing the splendid works of the mediaeval times, possibly

[1] *The Building News*, June 26th, 1872.

succeeding generations might have been fascinated by his works, and awed by the greatness of his name. But this modern British public, phlegmatic and unmovable in most things—always so in art matters—has not yet been educated up to his standard. In many of the great competitions of late years, men of eminence and large retaining fees have placed him highest on the list of competitors, but public opinion, like that embodiment at Covent Garden Theatre, shuts its eyes to the beauty of exterior show, tinsel, or glitter, which it confounds with true and noblest art. It looks at ease, comfort, mere arrangement and convenience as things of much greater importance, so that E. W. G. with his architecture always beautiful, and frequently unique, finds himself quietly shifted off the stage and pooh-poohed into the background." In flowery words, the writer of this letter puts the reason for the constant refusal to build the buildings designed by Godwin chosen by professional assessors. In plain English it was because the untrained layman on any committee could upset the considered award of the assessor. The latest example of this rejection had been the competition for St. Ann's Heath Lunatic Asylum, in which Godwin had had two designs selected.

One of his contributions upon " Modern Architects " of more importance in the present connection than the rest was about the work of Burges and himself. *The Times* had just dealt with their careers and work, which the writer said was " conceived in the most exclusive and enthusiastically mediaeval spirit ". It was to this article that he replied as if he were a stranger :

" Mr. Godwin's error is of a different kind, he starts from the same strong faith in early thirteenth-century work, but his vision is as too far-sighted as that of Mr. Burges is too near-sighted ; he dwells so long and so hypercritically on proportion and mass that he has no time left for detail, and thus with one exception—Northampton Town Hall—all his works suffer from blank spaces. They look, indeed, as if they had been designed with scissors instead of the pencil— for distant observation rather than for close examination. One could imagine that, feeling disgusted (and not without reason) at the manner in which his first highly decorative work

was executed, he had ' sworn off ' as Rip Van Winkle would
say and was growing cynical towards the sculptor or carver.
Be that as it may, I for one cannot help thinking that some of
his later works would have been all the better for a little of
those ornamental accessories which Mr. Godwin seems to
scorn. With these added, and something taken off the solids
and given to the voids, considerable gain would be effected.
But while saying this, I am quite conscious that this over-
attention to mass has been brought about by other architects
in the contrary direction. The excess of weakness in so many
modern works has driven Mr. Burges to the opposite extreme
of unmeaning strength ; the excess of fenestration has driven
Mr. Godwin to a spartan-like severity, which is certainly
not in harmony with the spirit of the age. The architecture
of the first reminds us of a Doric column reduced to half
its lowest height, that of the last, of a Corinthian without
its acanthus. We ask the one to be more graceful ; we ask
the other to be less severe . . ."

thereafter he concludes :

" Such are the opinions I have heard retailed in more or less
roundabout language. I suppose that I ought not to give an
opinion of my own one way or another. That I should have
taken the trouble to write them down may be considered bad
taste. Let it be so. There is so much good taste visible everywhere, so much modesty, so much consistency, that I shall not
mind the impeachment for the sake of the change."[1]

In another of this same series of articles he observes of Gothic :
" An architecture for churches is too like a religion that is only
for Sundays."
    In the field of design Edward had drawn various patterns for
wall papers for Jeffrey and Co. of which it was remarked, " Mr.
Godwin has gone beyond most people's notions of the bound-
aries of civilisation and has added Japan ". One of his suggestions
consisted of sunflowers, another of birds in flight, and the rest of
interlaced bamboo. Although he liked plain walls decorated in

[1]*The Building News*, p. 167, Vol. XXIII.

soft shades, finding them restful, he was willing to try to use the same tints in a design for a generation so fond of pattern. It was Metford Warner who persuaded him to try his hand in this most interesting art, and he was one of that far-seeing gentleman's most able discoveries in the year 1866, when Mr. Warner joined Jeffrey and Co. and set about revitalising the character of pattern, colour and printing processes.

Nor was this all. Since 1868, when he designed a coffee table, he had designed furniture for William Watt, by whom it was made and sold. The same maker made his own furniture. Now, for a friend of Ellen—Dr. George Bird of Welbeck Street—he designed three bookcases, a pair with painted " classic panels by a very brilliant young artist named Charles Glidden, who died when he was twenty ". The themes illustrated were Jason, Medea, Acteon, Hercules, and Aesculapius. The other, a desk-bookcase, was decorated by Jane Escombe with delicate leaf panels of herbs in the Japanese manner he admired so much.

The house at Harpenden—Fallows Green—was now built and furnished and the family moved into it. The ménage had been increased by the birth of a son a year before, and augmented by " Bo "—Miss Bocking—as nurse to the children. This young woman was the niece of " Boo ". Fallows Green was an ambitious venture, a large house set in twenty acres of ground. It has unfortunately been altered, having been coated with roughcast, and internally the staircase has been replaced by another. In consequence the Japanese character of the original is obliterated. The decorative scheme was similar to and the furniture the same as, the house in Bristol. Ellen wore " blue and white cotton ", and her daughter was dressed " in a kimono, in which she looked as Japanese as everything which surrounded her ".

As soon as the family had settled in Fallows Green, the subject of the £600 for furniture was again raised by Henry Crisp. In the eyes of Crisp and his lawyer the payment was now considered to be " payment you may have received for any professional services rendered during our partnership ", Crisp therefore being entitled to " a moiety of the sums in question ", the suggestion that there had been any impropriety about the payment having been withdrawn. Godwin replied to this letter

WALLPAPER, *The Peacock*.

by return of post—" I deny first of all having received any monies
due to the partnership which have not been put into my account ".

To this Henry Crisp, having consulted his lawyer, replied—
" you have not put into your account :

From the contractor for Dromore Castle   £600.
From the architects of the Plymouth Guildhall £100.
From Mr. Burgess [sic] if not in cash its equivalent, £100."

A share of these sums was deemed by Crisp's lawyer to be due
to Crisp since he considered them partnership monies. Godwin
and his lawyer thought differently and Crisp requested that the
question be referred to an arbitrator. Whether this course was
ultimately adopted is not known—nor how the argument was
settled. A little later Godwin referred in an interview to his
having earned the money by designing furniture—at home. That
he had designed Plymouth Guildhall and helped Burges was
public knowledge. He never hinted that there had been any dispute about the distribution of the £600. The only indication that
the claim may have gone against Godwin is that he raised money
by mortgage of Fallows Green and this may have been used
to settle with his partner. Thereafter the dispute was never again
mentioned—though the subject matter of all three claims was
talked about freely and openly by Godwin, who admitted to
having been paid for his services.

In the absence of the original of the partnership deed it is not
possible to decide which of the partners was in the right. Their
lawyers were at variance. It had been Godwin's contention that
the architect should be responsible for the design of the contents
of his buildings—he had claimed this a few days before he
entered into partnership—it is therefore probable that their
agreement contained a clause dealing with the subject. Helping
Norman and Hine was plainly architecture.

Although the issue was raised when the partnership was
about to expire it was not the cause of the dissolution. The
partnership terminated when the original agreement came to
an end.

The difference over the money, however settled, strained, but
did not alter, their relations. Their temperaments were very
distinct. Godwin clear, calm and certain and Crisp careful,

methodical, kindly, the soul of honesty and candour. When hard pressed they reacted differently—Godwin sometimes retorting by an obstinate indifference—or fatalism ; let what was coming take its course, he was right, he would never admit to error—unless he was judge of his own cause. Then, if he condemned himself, he published the findings. In the same sort of circumstances Henry Crisp was much disturbed. He took everything to heart. When the walls of Glenbegh let in the water, he wrote to all the firms he could discover in his anxiety to find a remedy. When Edward was informed he did not take any action—nor lose a night's sleep. By Crisp his inertia could only be comprehended as due to his " chronic ill-health ". Actually it was a consequence of his overwhelming self-reliance.

From now on, except for church and university building, Gothic was gradually discarded, or, if retained, was handled by the more able exponents in a freer manner. For church work, the use of revived mediaeval art was deemed by the Establishment to be inevitable.

That this was so the limited competition for a cathedral in Edinburgh evidenced. Six architects, three Englishmen and three Scotsmen, were invited to submit designs to the promoters. The names of the three former were Scott, Street, and Burges. Among the Scotsmen was Alexander Ross.

In Godwin's office at 29 Craven Street at the time, helping him as an assistant, was a young man, George Freeth Roper. Roper was a very brilliant draughtsman who had made a study of the work of Street, Burges and Godwin. He was able to design in the manners peculiar to them, and his drawings were only recognisable as not their work because he repeated their features.

Before the competition drawings were commenced, Ross came up to town and arranged that Roper should assist him to prepare the drawings for the Cathedral. On this visit he produced a rough sketch of his conception. Thereafter Roper was occupied in working up a drawing for the west front which, when completed, he showed to his employer Godwin. The rest of the drawings were made in Scotland by Alexander Ross's own staff.

When the award was made known, the design by Gilbert Scott was selected as the best, that by Alexander Ross as the second best. The high place awarded to Ross's design came as a shock to the big three and their admirers. A writer who reviewed the competition drawings in the press suggested that the design submitted by Ross was not his own work. Mr. Ross promptly replied that it was. A lengthy and acrimonious discussion followed upon the disputed authorship. Ross claimed that the original idea shown by him at the outset to Roper was his own and that all Roper had done was draw it out in greater detail; Roper said that the design had been made by him.

The evidence advanced in support of their claims, by each side, was inconclusive. Roper's work was clearly derived from a study of the mannerisms of Street, Burges and Godwin; he admitted as much himself. The design for the cathedral included vestiges of each of these designers' work, an amalgam that Ross could quite easily have suggested.

One of the few temperate contributions to the discussion came from Huskinson Guillaume, who pointed out that a drawing is not a design, that under certain circumstances neither Ross nor Roper could claim to be the author. It must be admitted that examples of the previous work of the disputants point to Roper as the author of the commended design. The case for Ross rested upon the willingness of some witnesses he had, prepared to swear that the sketch he had made before he ever saw Roper was like that ultimately commended. The dubious value of this evidence consisted in the fact that his witnesses were not architects, and might in such a matter of recollection have been mistaken, all Gothic appearing to the layman as alike. Edward waxed furious over this affair. He was certain that Alexander Ross was sailing under false colours, and that it was the Barry-Pugin situation over again. Save Roper and Ross, he knew as much as anyone, and was probably correct in his assumption for the drawing had been made in his office.

The issue never came before any court of law for resolution, though the accusers did their utmost to provoke Ross to action. Eventually both sides grew confused and the subject was dropped.

Naturally Ellen's day at Fallows Green was fully occupied in looking after the house, her children and Edward. As a relief, in August the year following, they went on a holiday in France.

They crossed to Normandy and visited and stayed in Bayeux, Lisieux and St. Lô.

At Bayeux Godwin discovered an armorie which he measured, noting in detail each of the fourteen doors in turn; describing the framework: " the post and rail decoration is painted in black ground, letting the white plaster form the pattern; and the margins in all save the large end-post are painted in red in the plaster, but no red is visible on the end-post, except beneath the plaster. Red, white and grey are used in the central finial with black scribbles on the white, and brown on the red; whilst green, red and golden yellow (with scribbles) occur on the end finials ". This is but a fragment of the commentary he wrote on the spot.

Of the celebrated tapestry he made a very detailed examination, and was specially interested in the sections referring to Godwin, Earl of Wessex. At Lisieux and St. Lô his sketch-book was brought out and filled.

" I always carry one of Henry Penny's Patent measuring 6 × 3¼ inches No. L.136 working with a very fine metallic point, and drawing as delicately and finely as I can." At all these resorts Ellen climbed the church towers and thoroughly enjoyed her architectural adventure.

When they got back home, Edward found an invitation to write about the work of the architect, Norman Shaw. At this moment Shaw had drawn much attention to himself on account of his recently completed New Zealand Chambers. Shaw was an older man than Godwin, but although his senior, had come into prominence later. He was a stranger to Edward, who confessed that so far as he was aware, he had never seen him. He made this admission in order to reassure his readers that his views were without prejudice. Of Shaw's houses, he believed that Preen and Leyes Wood were the better. Harrow Weald and Cragside " seem to me disjointed, each looks as if two or three houses had been brought together and shuffled up somehow into one ". Present-day opinion would no doubt support his judgement in so far as the composition of both these buildings is considered. Of the sensation of the day, New Zealand Chambers, Leadenhall Street, he admitted the colour to be charming. His criticism of the building is worth recall. In his opinion the cornice projected too far, and the detail of its soffit seemed too coarse, he did not like the pediments over the oriels, and felt that the elevation would have been improved if the dividing piers had been omitted.

If the last suggestion were carried out, the design would be a different one. There is more to be said for some of his other suggestions ; they are refinements which might improve without altering the total conception. While he was rather dogmatic in some of his views and wrote a great deal about other people, some of whom he had no cause to like, he always expressed himself in a detached manner. Watts's work, when he wrote of his painting, was not involved in Watts's actions. A noticeable feature of Edward's criticism of Shaw's or any other architect's work is that he never suggested that it originated from a study of his contemporaries. There were frequently cases in which the ideas of others were used without acknowledgement by in- different designers ; Shaw and Godwin had both been the victims of their own creative ability. Clearly this so prevalent plagiarism was a phase of the imitative cult which dominated the arts of nineteenth-century architecture and painting.

The entire lack of understanding of the creative artist is preserved in the words of the anonymous writers who, employed to explain the latest developments, spent their ink in trying to discredit them. The Whistler Show at the Dudley Gallery offered a suitable theme. For Godwin it had a special interest, as James McNeill Whistler—to whom he had been drawn on account of their common interest in Japanese art—was an exhibitor. They had been friends for some years, meeting frequently at the Arts Club and at their studios.

In the comment on the Dudley Show, the first artist to be sneered at was Legros. Next a *Harmony in Blue Grey* of the Thames was stigmatised. " It is nothing more than a very worth- less sketch, very impertinently treated. Here is the influence of Whistler's symphonies in jam and pomatum, nocturnes in pease puddings and carraways, variations in what you will." These pleasantries were not directed against Whistler, but against his assistant, Henry Greaves. When it came to the turn of the Master—Whistler's own *Variations in Pink and Grey*—" Why not brimstone and treacle?" exclaimed the elegant authority. Nor was this vulgarity confined to the anonymous, Burnand, the editor of *Punch*, and Harry Furniss excelled themselves: "Well, sir, I'm Master Jimmy Whistler, I am, and I can do this sort o' thing with a shilling box o' paints from the Lowther Arcade, a few sheets of blotting paper, and some brown paper covers off the family jam pots. I could do bigger work with improved materials, you bet!"

This quotation is but a mild example of the type of writing which passed for wit, to which the creative artists or architects— they numbered less than the fingers of a hand—were subjected. Fortunately for the reputation of English criticism, Edward Godwin shared neither their views of art nor their verbiage. His grounds of judgement were aesthetic, not associative.

Most of Edward's spare time during the year 1873 had been spent with Ellen at Harpenden upon a close study of each of Shakespeare's plays. To all appearances the couple seemed established in their way of life. True, for some unknown reason their finances were not in very good order. Expenditure had exceeded income, and to redress this the brokers had taken possession of the furniture in the house.

Where personal expenditure was involved, neither of them was cautious. Godwin had never been unemployed, nor was he solely dependent upon architecture for a living. He never referred to his money difficulties. On the other hand he did explain how simple it was to earn large sums from commercial art. Architects were in a different case. Fees for architectural service, based as they were on the cost of works, which with such low wages as then obtained, permitted very elaborate detail involving a great amount of labour and time spent on drawing, were small. The fact that Godwin had been highly praised by Eastlake in his *History of the Gothic Revival* had made little impression upon the layman. Further, the revival was at the ebb. Domestic expenditure was increasing—still, all in all, it is difficult to divine what was the real cause of the trouble evidenced by the presence of the sheriff's officers in the house.

Despite the disappointment over the break in his competition successes to all outward seeming he was happy. Quite naturally

Ellen, now twenty-five, was worried. The future of the children had to be thought about. Watts showed not the least intention of relenting. He had not used the opportunity to divorce his wife when the elopement took place, nor had the appearance of children altered his attitude. Time was slipping away. Small wonder that when it was too late he admitted that he had ruined his wife's life; his conduct had been without excuse.

The Christmas number of *The Graphic* for 1872 had contained a story by Charles Reade which was read by the family in Harpenden with personal interest, and was to have more. Ellen had performed in several of Reade's plays. She knew him well. It had been in one of them that she had made her last appearance on the stage. The story, *The Wandering Heir*, was based on the Tichbourne Case which was then exercising public feeling. As was Reade's habit he had turned the events into a story, and the story into a play. It was one of the peculiarities of the Victorian playwright that he was always attempting to turn the written word into the spoken word.

" *The Wandering Heir* was an exceedingly stagey production, containing the Shakespearian conception of a female character disguised as a man, with the common type of melodramatic ruffians and stage hypocrites."[1]

The author, Reade, was a big, bearded, boisterous bachelor. In addition to his fellowship of Merton he had earned large sums by the success of two of his novels, *It's Never too Late to Mend*, and *The Cloister on the Hearth*, and a number of less familiar stories and several plays. With the Terrys' old friend, Tom Taylor, Reade had collaborated in *Masks and Faces* and *Two Loves and Life*—both lively plays.

One day in the autumn of 1873 Ellen was driving through the country lanes with her children. She had nothing more in mind than her constant brooding upon the future, most particularly that of her children. Without warning, her reveries were broken when the wheel of the trap fell off suddenly, and the pony and trap were brought to a halt. The animal remained still, and happily none of them were hurt. Ellen got down and stood in the roadway, perplexed, wondering what to do, when suddenly

---

[1] *The British Architect*, May 29th, 1874, p. 342.

a crowd of horsemen scrambled over the fence into the road. Most of them hurried on after the fox, but one of them, a heavily-built, bearded man, reined in his mount and called out, " Can I be of any assistance ? " Then looking hard at her the rider exclaimed, " Good God! It's Nelly! Where have you been all these years ? " The more polite horseman was Charles Reade, who, like Anthony Trollope, was an enthusiastic follower of hounds. Ellen told him that she had been enjoying a country life. Whether she had been enjoying life or not, Reade thought it was high time that she returned to the stage and bluntly said as much. " No, never! " she declared.

But Charles Reade was not being dissuaded so easily. The encounter seemed providential for him. He was in need of a leading lady and here she was standing forlorn in the road trying to refix a loose wheel to a dilapidated trap. His then pre-occupation was to secure an actress for *The Wandering Heir*. Although the play had failed in Liverpool, Leeds and York, Reade was certain that the failure was through no fault of its construction. He always was. He was convinced that, with an improved caste, in London it would be a huge success, and show the stupid provinces that they could not recognise a good thing.

To put the matter to the test, he had resolved that he would stage the play at the Queen's Theatre, Long Acre. So far he had not found a suitable actress, and now that he had come upon Ellen so fortunately he was determined to secure her help. " You're a fool! " he retorted.

This rough remark provoked the recollection of the men in possession of the furniture, and she temporised :

" I might think of it if someone would give me forty pounds a week! "

" Done! " shouted Reade.[1]

[1]Ellen Terry's *Memoirs*, and *Charles Reade*, John Coleman. 1904. p. 329.

CHAPTER VII

A HOUSE IN LONDON

APPARENTLY Edward had no objections to offer either to Ellen's return to the stage or to the abandonment of a country life. Indeed, from his appreciative remarks, he seems to have favoured the idea. It would at least put an end to the gossip that he was standing in the way of her return to the theatre, and perhaps in London life for her would not be so lonely. Financially it would have been mere obstinacy to reject such an opportunity. His daughter was growing up, and her preliminary schooling would be more easily obtained in or near London than in rural Harpenden. Thus, though not without regret, the family moved to town, Edward, Ellen and her friend Boo, the two children and their nurse Bo. They took up residence in Taviton Street, Gordon Square.

At the same time Edward made another move, leaving his Craven Street office for rooms in 6 John Street, Adelphi, not far from the chambers of J. F. Bentley. What happened to the brokers at Fallows Green is of little moment. The furniture was redeemed—the house was his for two years longer.

Still troubles had not ceased. In the post, re-addressed from Craven Street, there arrived at his new quarters a writ from the solicitors for the owner of Glenbegh, Roland Winn. He posted the documents at once to Crisp in Bristol, as he had been instructed, but within a week they were back in John Street with a letter from his partner, who had had a similar service, telling him that if he " did not take *immediate* action in the matter, judgement will go against you by default ". Edward, designing a town hall for Sunderland, could not be bothered with writs, and passed on the news to Lane, his solicitor.

The dispute over Glenbegh Towers had monopolised far too much of Henry Crisp's time ever since the house had been completed in 1871, just after the end of the partnership. Winn and his lawyers had been persistently threatening to sue the firm for damages. The first complaint that the cost had exceeded the estimate having been discovered to be due to Winn, the threat was changed to the defective construction of the walls in consequence of which, it was stated, wet penetrated. This in turn was abandoned, and now that the actual charge was launched, it was the slating of the roofs which was at fault. It was late in September 1872, when J. T. Fuller, a Dublin architect who had inspected the buildings for Mr. Winn, came to this conclusion.

Although following the dissolution of partnership, the client had chosen to continue with Godwin as his architect, it was upon Crisp that the work fell. He had superintended the building, whereas Godwin—whose preoccupation was with Dromore—had only visited the place three or four times, Crisp had nearly all the correspondence and accounts in his keeping.

Now that the dispute had at last come to a head, Crisp wrote to Godwin suggesting that either J. P. Seddon or William Burges should be asked to make an independent survey of the work. Edward chose Seddon. At the end of September, Seddon and Crisp set out together from Bristol by packet to Cork, and thence through Killarney to Glenbegh. On arrival Henry Crisp, who from Fuller's report had anticipated finding the building in a bad state, wrote, " to my astonishment and satisfaction I found it quite the reverse ", and his companion Seddon made a report exonerating the architects.

Nothing more was heard from the owner's side until at the end of May 1873 Crisp told Seddon, " Winn is cropping up nasty again ", and in June the long-threatened proceedings again appeared imminent. Very alarmed, Crisp wrote urgently to T. H. Wyatt, Ewan Christian, R. W. Edis and several more architects asking them if they would join Mr. Seddon as witnesses if at liberty, when the case came before the courts—each of whom replied that he would, if he conscientiously could, give his aid.

From the moment when Winn first had threatened proceedings, Godwin had said he would not defend himself, and he remained throughout indifferent to the course of the case. Probably he had been advised by his solicitor, Lane, to take no notice of the threats and charges, and to maintain a discreet silence until a formal claim was made by the Hon. Roland Winn. Possibly the fact that Winn had insulted him made him all the more determined to let the client do his worst—and be damned! Yet although Winn and he had become reconciled, Edward still persisted in his refusal to defend the action. That was the situation in 1874 when the claim was at long last formulated. Crisp had given up any hope of a united front and had parted from Godwin's solicitor and engaged a Bristol lawyer—his friend Freddie Harwood. In any event, Edward's " chronic ill-health " precluded his visiting Ireland or giving evidence in that country.

Both parties now engaged Dublin lawyers, and the issue rapidly developed. Winn had demanded £5,000, an obviously impossible sum to sustain. The opposing lawyers conferred, with the result that a meeting was arranged of Winn and Crisp in London. There is no doubt that Winn had been told by his adviser to accept Crisp's offer, " my proposal being to do the necessary work of the house myself, or otherwise pay an equivalent in money ". Winn replied, " That is all I can expect ". The upshot was that in April 1874 an agreement was signed and the whole dispute ended " once and for all ".

What part Godwin played in the final agreement is in doubt. Perhaps at the last moment he had acquiesced in some arrangement whereby Crisp became the sole defendant, for it is reputed that Edward contributed to the costs of the settlement. Unsatisfactory as it may have seemed, the final agreement was doubtless the most economical for both disputants. Winn could never have expected to succeed in his exorbitant claim, and if he had persisted, he would have been mulched in costs. At all stages of the trouble Crisp had vacillated between defence and compromise. It was only when the case was put into the hands of Irish solicitors, who between them formulated a compromise, that Crisp could accept.

The cost of repairing the roof cannot have been great, but the costs of the law were considerable.

While this dispute was engaging nearly all Henry Crisp's attention, Edward and his dependants were trying to adjust themselves to their new surroundings in Taviton Street. If these legal transactions troubled Godwin at all, he did not show his feelings. Instead, as soon as the decision to move to London was made, he arranged for the decoration of his new home, a matter of much greater interest to him than the Hon. Roland Winn's action. The scheme for the drawing-room impressed callers so deeply that, like Forbes-Robertson, they remembered it ever after. " The floor was covered with straw-coloured matting, and there was a dado of the same material. Above the dado were white walls and the hangings were of cretonne, with a fine Japanese pattern in delicate grey-blue. The chairs were of wicker with cushions like the hangings, and in the centre of the room was a full size cast of Venus de Milo, before which was a small pedestal, holding a censer from which was, curving round the Venus, ribbons of blue smoke."[1]

Into this room Ellen would glide in her amazing grace, dressed in a blue kimono in harmony with the colour scheme of the room. It was in this setting that she received Forbes-Robertson, a young artist about to turn actor, who had called to discuss the play in which, with her, he was due to appear.

Edward believed in the force of example. He could not bear to live surrounded by the cumbersome furniture of the 'seventies, nor would he tolerate the corseted, bustled costumes worn by the fashionable. His callers thought him eccentric, not understanding why any normal person should be distressed by shapes and colours, or so absurd as to design ladies' or children's dresses. They were amazed that Ellen should wear such queer confections, yet they had to admit reluctantly that when she wore them her elegance was such as they had never before encountered. The ménage could only be understood when one realised that these two odd creatures were artists, unaccountable to plain, ordinary folk.

Charles Reade, himself a character (his mistress having suffered from rheumatism, he buried her, when she died, in a brick vault in order that she should not feel the cold), was puzzled. After he had engaged Ellen to play he wrote in his

[1] *A Player under Three Reigns*, Robertson, p. 66.

B

diary : " She is an enigma. Her eyes are pale, her nose rather long, her mouth nothing particular. Complexion a delicate brick dust, her hair is rather like tow. Yet somehow she is beautiful. Her expression kills any pretty face beside her. She is a pattern of fawn-like grace. Whether in movement or repose, grace pervades the hussy. In character—impulsive, intelligent, weak, hysterical, in short all that is abominable and charming in a woman."[1]

She had been away from the stage for a long time, and when she had quitted it, had been little known and quite overshadowed by her sister. Nor were her potential qualities realised, save in his intuitive fashion by the dramatist Charles Reade. But neither Watts nor Edward, Taylor nor Reade had guessed at what was hidden in her future.

It was in February 1874 that the day for Ellen's return to the theatre arrived. *The Wandering Heir*, in which she played the part of Phillipa Chester, was produced to show what a good play it was ; to enable the enthusiastic author to say " I told you so! " It had failed dismally in the provinces, and on its London opening the critics damned the show with faint praise :

> " It would be almost wearying to sit it out, even if every actor in it were equal to Miss Terry. So long as she is on the stage notably in the fourth act, time passes quickly and pleasantly. . . . Miss Terry is so well known and so highly appreciated by old theatre-goers that it will be sufficient to say that her performance in this piece is one of the most graceful and natural effects it has ever been our good fortune to witness."[2]

The actor who played the part of James Annesley, Johnston Forbes-Robertson, was singled out as specially able by the writer, who was none other than Edward Godwin, a spectator in London, who later saw the production in the country.

The two—Robertson and Ellen—made the play. Notwithstanding the animadversions of the press, it suited the taste of the moment in London, and the tense interest in the Tichbourne Case aided the success. In fact, *The Wandering Heir* confounded

[1]*Charles Reade*, John Coleman, 1904, p. 329.
[2]*The British Architect*, May 29th, 1874, p. 342.

everybody except the author, and ran to packed houses for one hundred and thirty nights—or as long as the theatre could be retained.

When it was withdrawn, Reade took Ashley's and, with Ellen as his leading lady, produced *It's Never too Late to Mend*. The revival of his standby was not appreciated. Undismayed, Reade transferred *The Wandering Heir* with the entire London company to the country.

Edward, the children and their nurse, remained in town. The building trade was very quiet and he had little architectural work in hand. His most important duty was the job of advising the architects, Hine and Norman, at Plymouth Town Hall. There is no doubt that he felt this neglect very deeply. "That independence which is always present in the real artist, whether working or waiting for work, prevents him as a rule from hiring himself out at a fixed rate," was how he reflected. At the same time he deplored the neglect of the architect— "founded on the erroneous supposition that the importance of a thing is in exact proportion to its cost, which in spite of our desire to make it so, it is not, never has been, and never will be ". He would rather give a design than work on a percentage of its cost of execution. He had just been awarded two premiums for Sunderland Municipal Buildings.

This moment was selected by the editor of *Women and Work*, Emily Faithful (an early advocate of the emancipation of women), as a suitable occasion upon which to approach Godwin for his views on the prospect of women as architects! He accepted the invitation, writing wholeheartedly in favour of their entering the profession, for which he explained they were naturally fitted. The one essential qualification was " accuracy and repose is desirable ". Undoubtedly he had the memory of Ellen tracing Burges' extravagant Cardiff details, when he penned the next few words, " and of that equipoise which is indispensable for the creation of beauty ". His own momentary worries also intruded. After this temperamental introduction, he proceeded to explain the many kinds of outlets there were for an architect, including a list of types of buildings, and ending, " Private Houses, Monuments, Illustration of Old Works, Cabinet work, Metal work,

Carpets and Hanging, Paintings on Cabinets, Painting on Walls and Ceilings, Wall paper design, Tiles ", as the main probable employments for a woman. All the last could, he explained, be designed at home. His enthusiasm must have made some of the young women who read his words eager to become architects.

Male members of the calling were not enthusiastic, and the misogynists said the suggestion was preposterous, although there was nothing in the Charter of the Royal Institute of British Architects that precluded women from membership. To support his theories, Godwin took a lady pupil.

It was high time for change—change in costume both male and female, ways of life, furniture, position of women, conception of the beautiful and of material things, lighting, heating, communications, transport. In all the arts the romantic movement was on the wane, and the modern idiom had been born. It dawned upon some of the creative minds that there was a life about them which was passing unregarded by the painters, poets, playwrights, novelists and architects.

Reade had a dim notion of this, but his method of dealing with urgent themes was infected by a backward looking, and his novels were overloaded by the result of research and description of scenery. His use of his stories as plays was a pale repetition of the method by which Shakespeare had constructed his histories. All the writers for the theatre were similarly persuaded until one of them, T. W. Robertson, wrote *Society* and the comedies which led up to and culminated in *Caste*. This last play was an attempt to put life as it is before the audience, free from exaggeration of plot, sound and fury that had served for drama. In a quiet, naturally constructed play he revealed to the audience that the conventions of the day contained as moving material as the past.

Indirectly, Robertson's plays furthered a similar decline in the importance attached to spectacular scenery and effects ; these had gradually monopolised the theatre until the reality of rivers, lakes and waterfalls had eliminated the need for any intelligence in the play. In the presentation of *Caste* it was the little things which mattered, the ceiling of the room, the locks on the doors, the furniture and its arrangements.

In the larger field of architecture there were indications of a parallel movement. Avern's house and Norman Shaw's New Zealand Chambers, though not the earliest, were preliminary indications of the trend toward the reconciliation of nineteenth-century men and buildings. In effect, the revival of Queen Anne's architecture was the counter-attack of the devotees of classic architecture, who had been forced to retreat before the Gothic hosts in the battles of the styles. The architectural retort was less complete than the dramatic, though to antiquarians it seemed to be revolutionary. It was still backward looking, but the distance was less.

Oddly enough the London School Board was the body that initiated the most conspicuous examples of modernity. The change was brought to the notice of architects at their Conference in London in 1874. The architect who introduced the discussion was J. J. Stevenson, whose right to talk on the subject was that he had built himself a house—The Red House, Bayswater—and had revived the renaissance for its fashioning. He had helped and was still helping Robson, the School Board architect, to design some of the many schools in the Queen Anne manner. Stevenson was a Scotsman, an able architect, but a queer character. His habit was to carry about with him a bass which is said to have contained a towel, a piece of soap, a shirt and a small bottle of whisky. Such was the advocate of the Annites!

The paper he read to the Conference was entitled, *On the Recent Reaction of Taste in English Architecture*. He began by discussing the several suggested reasons why the change had come about that had superseded the Gothic revival. These were that the pre-Raphaelites had initiated it ; that the novels of Thackeray, Kingsley and Dickens had led to an interest in the Georges ; or that the Gothic revival had worked itself out. Stevenson dismissed them all as Aunt Sallies, and claimed that the style had been selected by the School Board architects because they had discovered " that Queen Anne and the Early Georges . . . form the nucleus of a modern style ", and continued : " The style in all its forms has the mark of truthfulness ; it is the outcome of modern wants picturesquely expressed."[1] His paper was the outstanding event of the Conference. It was the public début of

[1] *The Architect*, Vol. XII, 1874, p. 1.

a new movement, the leaders of which were nicknamed the
Annites by Mrs. Haweis.

For months afterward, the theme was the burning question for
discussion in the building papers. The Annites were the more
numerously vocal, the Gothic less numerous, less argumentative,
but more abusive. What may be called the old guard, Street,
Burges and lesser-known Lacy Ridge (who figures in J. D.
Beresford's *House Mates*), had nothing good to say for a manner
of building which they despised.

If any man may be singled out as the leader of the Annites in
the days of discussion which followed the Conference, the credit
should be given to Professor Robert Kerr. Kerr was rash enough
to say, " if there was a competition just now for such a building
as the Law Courts, we can readily enough imagine that half the
number of designs, or possibly the whole, might be in one form or
another of the Queen Anne Style." Street was furious.

Some weeks later, Kerr gave the movement a new title;
Stevenson and others had thought the name Queen Anne
inappropriate, but had failed to suggest any alternative. Kerr
dubbed it the Modern European Style, and was exceedingly proud
of the new designation which he claimed to have coined in 1857.

It had happened in this way. Mr. Kerr as a young man had
been one of a deputation led by William Tite and Professor
Donaldson to interview Lord Palmerston when his lordship
was trying to get a classic design for the Foreign Office from
G. G. Scott. Anxious to aid Palmerston young Kerr had blurted
out : " What you require is something in the Modern European
Style."

" Ha, ha! " chuckled his Lordship. " That's it! "

Kerr now recalled with pride the approbation of the great man.
And as if he had grown tired of waiting for the style's appearance,
he now proclaimed : " The time seems to have come, as it does
now and then, for some sort of new school to appear."

The mention of the Law Courts provoked Mr. G. E. Street,
never a polite controversialist, to write of Kerr : " He has
done nothing. Never been abroad. Writes too much on too
many subjects. A critic should practise what he preaches."
Then he composed the poor epigram, " Queen Anne Street leads

naturally to Harley Street ". Not undeservedly, Street met with the fate of the man who interferes in a fight; the combatants ceased fighting each other and attacked him.

Edward did not take part directly in the dispute; he had already adopted the new manner and, so far as the design of furniture was affected, had long practised the theory, once more stated by his friend John Seddon, that if they would " prohibit the use of a single detail, the purpose of which in the construction could not be satisfactorily explained, or of any ornament which did not express some fact or thought worth record, architects would have to seek effect, as they should, in form, outline, proportion, dispositions and shape of openings . . . and we should soon be on the right road to a modern European style ".

Removal to London and Ellen's absence on tour gave Godwin more time to visit the Arts Club of which he was a member. He could meet his friend, J. McNeill Whistler, and that remarkable factotum of uncommercial artists, Charles Augustus Howell. The club was then housed in the corner house, Tenterden Street, Hanover Square, a beautiful Georgian town house, the first floor boasting two rooms, of which the ceilings were said to have been painted by Angelica Kauffmann.

Edward constituted himself a supporter of the American. They were natural allies, since each was an enthusiast for the Japanese perception of nature. In July 1874, Whistler held a show at 48 Pall Mall, at which his oils and etchings were exhibited, amongst these the portraits of Thomas Carlyle and the artist's mother. Of these the latter was preferred. The colour combination of the other pictures met with more approval than did their composition—the *Harmony in Flesh Colour and Pink* and in *Grey and Peach* particularly being deemed too straight in pose. *The Saverne*, a small room with a female figure looking out of a window, *The Parasol* and two others were admired.

The room in which they were hung was furnished in brown, with coloured screens and pottery giving it a house-like appearance. The two men had together made the arrangement. Whistler's pictures were made to live with.

Most of Edward's time during Ellen's absence on tour was, however, taken up in putting the finishing touches to a series of articles amounting to a book on *The Architecture and Costume of Shakespeare's Plays.*

They were the outcome of his lifelong study of the dramatist, his readings in Bristol and his talks with Ellen. Even after discounting some of the literary attributions of the originals of the plays as having been explored by previous scholars, there yet remains an immense volume of exposition contributed by him. Nobody had explained, as he did, the minutiae of setting and costuming. The number of references to books, pictures, buildings and the verbal allusions in the text of the plays to the scene and clothing of the characters, is proof of the care with which he had considered all the external evidence and the implication of each word in the plays. Obviously he had spent many hours in the study of the costumes depicted by the Italian masters contemporary with the action of the plays, or the effigies on tombs of the age of chivalry, and statuary or painting of Greece and Rome, taking note of all that would assist him in the undertaking. Occasionally the papers were subsequently made topical by the addition of a paragraph or more, bearing upon some incident that had occurred shortly before their publication.

In all there were thirty-three articles, quite a hundred thousand words. Not only scene, dress, furniture, but the manners and habitual actions of the characters in each period are explained. There was guidance for all the participants in the theatre—producer, actor, scene painter, furnisher and costumier. Nor was the play forgotten through over-interest in the spectacle.

When the writing and research were nearing their end, Ellen returned to Taviton Street. The provincial round of *The Wandering Heir* had not been the success anticipated after its rehabilitation in London. Her forty pounds a week ceased, and she had no further engagement in view. The scenery on tour had been in the old amusing careless style. In the act depicting the trial at the Old Bailey of James Annesley for murder, the court had been represented :

" Instead of this (the real Court), we are given a Gothic Church! Nothing more or less. There is the chancel arch, the Gothic chancel screen, and the east window of the chancel traceried and filled with painted glass, treated as a transparent background." No doubt it was assumed that few of the audience had ever seen the inside of the Old Bailey!

Unfortunately, Ellen's return was the signal for the brokers to thrust their company again upon the family. Probably they believed that there was a better chance of getting the money they claimed. The cause of the trouble is obscure, but most likely the rent or housekeeping accounts were in arrears, for Godwin was careless of his own affairs—in any case the visitors removed some of the furniture. This distraint had been often threatened, now it had been executed.

Friends urged Ellen to break with Edward, who was, they said, spoiling her chances. The most persistent advisers were Reade and Taylor who might have helped her. What benefit they imagined would accrue from a separation is not clear, since Godwin had not prevented her return to the stage—their great concern for her. She was undecided, for she loved him.

At this critical moment Ellen stood forlorn in the bare room. The hangings gone, the cretonne chairs gone, the matting left and she, enchanting as ever, dressed in a yellow and brown tabard, was alone with the Venus de Milo as cold company. What was that ? There came a knock at the door of the room and a voice called " May I come in ? "

Before she could answer, the door opened and a little lady dressed in black entered, glanced towards the statue, shaded her eyes as if shocked and exclaimed *sotto-voce*, " Dear me! "

Affecting to disregard the bleak state of the room, the lady, Mrs. Bancroft, for it was she who had made this unexpected entrance, began to explain that she and Squire Bancroft had decided to stage *The Merchant of Venice* at the Prince of Wales Theatre, and as she could not take the character part herself, would Ellen come to the rescue and play Portia ? " Mr. Godwin will be asked to control the artistic direction." No doubt the Bancrofts had heard of the articles on Shakespeare which, beginning with Hamlet, had begun to appear in print. Ellen agreed to help.

" My work will, I feel certain, be joyful work and joyful work should turn out good work."[1] So she wrote in her letter of acceptance of the part.

[1] *Gleanings*, Mrs. Bancroft, p. 176 ; or *On and Off the Stage*, p. 208, 1889.

CHAPTER VIII

THE MERCHANT OF VENICE

IN HIS *Architecture and Costume of Shakespeare's Plays*, Godwin had written at length upon *The Merchant of Venice*, as, indeed, he had upon each of the plays, although as yet only those articles dealing with *Hamlet, Romeo and Juliet, Cymebeline, Macbeth, King John, Richard II* and *Henry IV* had been published. That considering *The Merchant* did not appear until the staging of the Bancroft revival in which Ellen and he were engaged.

Edward began to work upon the production at once, consulting with Mr. Gordon, the scene painter, whom he despatched to Venice in December to obtain the necessary local colour. Ellen began her rehearsals.

The theatre, for the moment, was not his main preoccupation, for he was engaged as usual on a multitude of projects. Writing about Japanese art ; moralising upon the theatre ; hob-nobbing with Whistler at the Club ; and visiting all the art shows. At the Dudley Gallery, where he found most of the work " good ", he began his account of them and " their effect upon me ", by a description of himself as " an habitual grumbler and cantankerous critic . . . who desires for once to say something which I trust may be regarded as genuine praise ". With three exceptions, Holliday, Poynter and Severn, the artists, were unknown. As always, his comments convey intelligence of his character. " Personally I have a foolish prejudice against black skins ", follows his reference to a drawing of a group of negroes ; of *Sea Picture* he remarked that it was some time since he had seen either a " seascape or landscape " and had on this account found them pleasurable in watercolour. Of flower pieces, "Why will our flower painters not take a lesson or two from the Japanese, who in the art of flower-compositions are simply pre-eminent?" Only one of the painters in "the architectural group" found favour. "Arthur Severn is the only artist who attracts me. His work is faithful, and his buildings happen to stand upright."[1]

At home in Taviton Street he was occupied in the study of Japanese constructional principles. His text, "lying on the table as I write, a Japanese book: for all I know it may be quite a common collection of prints, or it may be out of print and rare." This book with fifty-six pages of illustration— "supplemented by reference to other native books and drawings, and to such photographs and illustrations as those I have by me" —provided his education in "the architectural characteristics of Japan".

Upon Japanese art, about which he was so great an authority and upon which his pioneer work in the modern idiom was founded, his words have interest.

"In art circles it is by no means uncommon to meet with people who, while they admit the fact that the Japanese are endowed with a keen sense of colour and with a great faculty for drawing natural objects, are yet rash enough to say that they have no knowledge of perspective, and are indifferent to beauty in human form. Such people, and there are many of them, judge the Japanese from the standpoint of a shop in Regent Street or Baker Street, and not infrequently from a still lower level, to wit, a few pans and trays picked up at their family grocers. Nothing can be more misleading than this, for one who is at all acquainted even in the smallest degree with the best class of Japanese work—and by work I do not mean a pan, or a tray, or a cabinet—can for a moment have any doubt as to the high artistic excellence which permeates the entire country."

Now that his début as, in part at least, a producer of a play drew nearer, he was occupied more and more in thinking about the implications of his devotion to the art. The news that he was embarking upon such a venture was viewed with dismay by his brethren, one of whom, W. H. White, wrote feelingly:

[1] *The Building News*, February 5th, 1875, p. 146.

" Whereas the loss to the profession of those who are continually crying out for better buildings and design, cannot be too highly estimated when the *most accomplished living architect in England is expending his tried powers over the trappings of a play.*"

Such expressions of opinion were growing year by year, having little regard for the fact that more significant buildings, if less notorious than Northampton Town Hall, came from his hand after his assumed abandonment of architecture than had issued before his immersion in theatrical production. He had a creative urge sufficiently intense to leave his mark on the other arts, major and minor. About the theatre, his opinion was : " It is only in the theatre that we see (or rather might see) the noblest results of civilisation. Poetry, music, architecture, painting, sculpture, meet in undisturbed harmony." " The attempt to revive either the glories of the Classic or Gothic art are impossible." The consequence could only be an incongruous set-scene, " as inconsistent as the Acropolis in *The Merry Wives of Windsor* or Westminster Abbey in *The Clouds* ". It was this obsession that alarmed his brethren.

He remembered that long ago in Bristol he had tried to express an " unprejudiced opinion . . . on the acting, scenery, properties, costume and (in a rash moment) the management of two of our provincial theatres ". His reward, a flogging. Writing about these details had had no hearing in London, for " the London theatres of to-day are wholly below the standard attained of those two provincial theatres ".

The actors were not to blame. He had singled out, more than ten years before, Kate Terry, Henrietta Hodson, Madge Robertson and Kate Bishop (then a child) as having great futures before them, and they had not failed, although the whole environment in which they had struggled had been hostile.

The Actor was regarded as a vagabond. The audience were said to be composed of persons of low mentality, and when some years earlier they had been criticised for their vulgarity— " some common-sense people suggested that it might be just as well, before we cried out upon their indecencies, to look to their dwellings and give them cottages which should afford them the chance of living a little better than a pig, perhaps, though not as good as a horse. With equal reason we may suggest an enquiry into the arrangement and construction of that miserable-looking portion of the theatre which lies behind the footlights ".

Here, in the most deplorable surroundings, scene painters, carpenters, modellers and dressmakers worked all day and half the night. " Here are the actor and actress for four or five hours every night, and often for an even longer time in the day." The entire environment had "a vicious influence, demoralising to the art, and disappointing to the artist". The money was expended on the wrong parts of the building. "I do not hesitate to say that the money expended on the vulgar ostentation displayed in the auditorium and public entrances would be more than enough to provide healthy, convenient, and even comfortable accommodation for those who minister to our amusement or instruction."

As an architect who was convinced that the external had a profound influence, and that the first thing needing attention was the building in every part, he wrote : " Another most objectionable arrangement often found in modern theatres is that of the stage entrance. For some reason best known to those who hold fast to stage traditions, the stage door is, as a rule, exceedingly narrow, and opens into a stuffy lobby, adjoining a still more stuffy porter's or doorkeeper's room ; occasionally the two are rolled into one, when, as a consequence, it possesses a double share of stuffiness, for here, sometimes alone, and sometimes with friends, the doorkeeper not infrequently regales himself on refreshments of a quality by no means so refined as to add any extra charm to that threshold where the histrionic Art is supposed to welcome her disciples."[1]

Edward went in and out through this stage door with more and more familiarity as the day of the opening, Saturday, drew nearer. He was supposed by his employers to be solely concerned about the coming spectacle as seen from the front. In order to realise his intention from this angle, a few words from his paper on *The Merchant of Venice* will serve to show his ideas and indicate the range of the rest of these remarkable essays.

After some preliminary discussion as to the probable date of the action of the play, he determined the period to be 1590,

[1] *The Building News*, March 19th, 1875, pp. 311–12.

although he adds : " The improbabilities, I may say the im-
possibilities, of these two fictions having any foundation in the
history of any European city during the sixteenth century are
self-evident. The very dawn of commercial enterprise would be
even too late for the two great barbaric events of the play—
the flesh forfeit and the trial by casket." He fixed the season of
the year as autumn.

" The architectural scenery, divided between Venice and
Belmont, may be said to consist at the most of five scenes, viz. :

VENICE   (1) A street or public place.
          (2) A street before Shylock's house.
          (3) A Court of Justice.
BELMONT   (4) A great hall.
          (5) A garden.

The first, i.e. the public place or street in Venice, might then
be planned as shown in the annexed diagram, when A is Shylock's
house ; B, the public place with a fountain or well ; C, canals ;
D, a pent house ; E, a narrow street ; F, Gothic and late Byzantine house ; G, a Renaissance public building with arcades ;
H, early Byzantine buildings ; M, N, the Proscenium. In such
a scene as this, of course, it is very evident that everything may
be built out."

Then he continued to discuss the actual architectural examples
appropriate : the pavement, and finally the colour of the scene.

" Let into this field of softened and almost neutral-toned
colour came the glistening white marble shafts and arches of the
windows, each window or group of windows framed by an edging
of marble. Gold was applied to such details as the cusps, the
carving and the edges of the mouldings ; bright bits of colour
nestled in the background of the sunk work, and not infrequently
medallions of porphyry and sepentine enriched the plain surfaces
between the arch line and the rectangular frame."

For the Court of Justice he suggested adapting the Sala della
Scrutinio.

" The setting of it on the stage is altogether another question,
and is one of the most difficult problems among the scenic

questions of Shakespeare's play. . . . Considering all the circumstances of the case, I again propose a diagonal set for this scene."

All the costumes to be worn are described in detail. Since Ellen was to play Portia, some of his remarks about her must serve for them all.

" Portia would do her shopping probably at Padua, and would therefore follow the fashions of the main-land. The chief difference we have to note is the absence of the square-cut body. High-necked bodies, with fine cambric ruffs, was the everyday attire usually worn by Paduan ladies of noble birth. On state occasions, on festivals and at receptions, the dress, though still high at the shoulders, was open in front, terminating at a point a little above the waist. There is also a marked difference to be observed between the dresses of a maiden and that of a married woman, and there is no question that the Paduan ladies (wives or not) indulged in a considerably extensive wardrobe. So, too, there was more than one mode of dressing the hair. In some cases it was crimped, parted in the middle, brought round to the back over the ears and rolled up *a la grie*, in others it fell loosely down the back *au natural*, confined, however, at the poll by a delicately wrought band or tiara of goldsmith's work ; but the more usual plan was to arrange the front hair in massive curls, assuming somewhat the form of a couple of low horns, and carried down each side in smaller curls to the ears, the hair behind strained (sometimes crimped and fastened up into a plait with strings of pearls interwoven). From this plait depended the veil, which sometimes appears to have covered the head up to a point between the horned curls or rolls, over which it could be raised like a double hood. The veil itself was also worn in various ways, and as it was only arranged with the utmost grace and made of the finest material—a sort of silken gauze, enriched with gold, interwoven and sometimes embroidered and decorated further with pearls and gems—its lovely film-like effect, like an iridescent mist over the rich materials of the gown, can better be imagined than described. The gown, with the exceptions already noted, was cut like the Venetian dress and was made of silk, brocade, gold cloth or costly velvet. Over the shoulders was worn a chain, usually of gold set with jewels and suspending a large jewel or cross. The pouch of gipcieve worn at the girdle was not quite yet abandoned, and Portia may wear one or not as she pleases. In addition to this, brides and married women wore a gold chain following the triangular lines of the waist and hanging down in front as low as the knee. Gowns with the skirt open up the front and with loose hanging sleeves were also used by the ' Spora de Padona '. Rings were worn on the first, third and fourth fingers. Ear-rings of pearls and jewels appear, and sometimes we see a string of pearls, one end attached to the ear and the other looped up to the back hair. The veil is occasionally omitted, and a stiff, semi-circular collar of lace is seen standing up behind the neck and reaching as high as the poll. Portia's stockings would be silk or the finest thread worked with clocks and even seams. Her shoes, of slipper form, would be of morocco or of velvet, embroidered with gold, cork being used for the soles. On her journey to Venice she would use a velvet mask or riser and gloves highly perfumed and embroidered with gold or silver. A pocket looking-glass, with ladies of rank, was not an uncommon possession, and was sometimes set in the back of the fan, which was usually made of nine or more ostrich feathers, the handle set with pearls and jewels and fastened to the end of the girdle chain of the lady who was married. The pocket handkerchief was of large size and of fine cambric, having an embroidered border and a tassel at each corner. . . ."

Very much more was written about Portia, including a description of the costume worn by a D.C.L. of Padua. In conclusion, Edward gave advice as to how all the actors should comport themselves in the several situations of the play.

He had spent hour after hour discussing the details of the presentation of all the plays of Shakespeare during the winter evenings in Harpenden and had enjoyed writing out the result of all this reflection and research when Ellen had been away in the north.

The Bancroft production was to be his opportunity. In a sense he had been preparing for the occasion since he was a small boy in Bristol, poring over his illustrated Planché and reading with Hine the magic words.

RHEINFIELDON, NORTHAMPTON.

BEDFORD PARK, CHISWICK.

For the Prince of Wales performances he carried realism to great lengths. In fact, the detail of costume and colour is far more precise than necessary for stage presentation.

"Elaborate capitals of enormous weight . . . were cast in plaster, and part of the wall of the theatre had to be cut away to find room for them to be moved by means of trucks on and off the stage . . ."[1] was how Lady Bancroft recalled the production when it had become a part of stage history. The diagonal set, which was a favourite of Edward's at this date, had originated in the mind of Charles Kean, or at any rate that he was the first actor-producer to use.

When the great day came Portia, in the casket scene, wore a dress like almond blossom, designed for her by Edward. She played the part slowly and stiffly, as he had advised. The moment she spoke the words, " You see me, Lord Bassanio, where I stand ", the house rose. " Never until I appeared as Portia at the Prince of Wales," wrote Ellen Terry, " had I experienced that awe-struck feeling which comes, I suppose, to no actress more than once in a lifetime—the feeling of the conqueror."

Her reception was tremendous : never throughout her subsequent career did she ever experience anything of like nature. The audience were spellbound. In an instant she had established herself as the greatest actress of her time.

Her success was no accident, for she had given the most careful study to her every accent and action. What was peculiar is that the role of Shylock, taken by Charles Coghlan, was indifferently played. He could not be heard. It came to be said in jest that it was *The Merchant of Venice* without Shylock.

Of the scenery William Henry White wrote in high commendation : " The second scene, representing an interior in Portia's house in Belmont, surpasses everything yet produced upon the English stage ; not for gorgeousness, nor size, nor any sensational belongings, but because it is a true picture of a stately hall, likely to have been erected by Portia's kinsfolk, two, or perhaps three, generations before her time."[2]

[1]*The Bancrofts, Recollections of Sixty Years*, 1909, p. 205.
[2]*The Building News*, April 23rd, 1875, p. 471.

About the costume of the play Mr. White was critical, prefacing his observations by saying : " With the costume, regarded archaeologically, it may reasonably be presumed Mr. Godwin, whose name is advertised as the archaeological adviser of the scene painter, had very little, if anything, to do." In truth, only some of the dresses worn by Portia were of Godwin's suggestion, and these met with White's approval. As her costume as an advocate was not that of a D.C.L. Padua but of a judge, Edward could not be blamed for the solecism. His part in the design of the costumes, other than those worn by Ellen, was confined to colour, of which the critic observed : " In no scene is there any jarring of colour."

To-day it is recognised that the return of Ellen, and the début of Godwin, marked the renaissance of theatrical art in England. The Bancroft company worked together as a team. No actor was unduly prominent and in consequence their productions were more balanced than those in which some familiar figure was encouraged to tower above the other players. The play did not run for very long owing to it having been produced early in the year and not in the autumn of the previous year, or, as some of the critics thought, because of the curious interpretation of the character of Shylock as an aged and feeble old man by Charles Coghlan.

Despite this withdrawal, the intelligentsia, now called by the newspapers " the aesthetes ", were in high feather. Among the first-night audience was a young undergraduate from Magdalen, Oscar Wilde, who was captivated by Ellen's personality and performance and could only find relief in a sonnet :

> " *For in that gorgeous dress of beaten gold,*
> *Which is more golden than the golden sun,*
> *No woman Veronese looked upon*
> *Was half so fair as thou whom I behold.*"

George Augustus Sala, who missed the first night, begged for seats for himself and his wife.

As yet Wilde was in thrall to the pre-Raphaelite preference for blue china and old oak, and his rooms were furnished in their fashion. Although at Oxford he was looked upon as a leader of a coming movement, in reality he was the inheritor of one outworn.

He had not until now met Edward, who, with Whistler, was eventually to give a twist to his views. Godwin was the exemplar in practice of the movement that Wilde was subsequently to adopt as his own.

When *The Merchant of Venice* had commenced its brief showing, Godwin made his only considered public reference to the " Queen Anne " debate which yet continued to interest the architects, and which had been further discussed two weeks earlier by Stevenson and Ridge.[1] There are two interesting remarks in his lengthy talk that may be quoted :

" If the ex-Classic of to-day is not big enough to embrace town halls and law courts, chapels and cathedrals, as well as suburban villas ; if it is not strong enough to influence the whole character of modern manufacture and make itself felt in the works of the potter, the glass makers, and the smith, in the looms of Yorkshire and Lancashire—in a word, if it has not vitality enough to permeate the whole body of Society, this last attempt will end, like so many others, in the merest sham, and this new endeavour to beget a living style must perforce prove futile."

And later :

" What then is left ? Nothing but the vernacular, the builder's work, naked of ornament, void of style, and answering only to one name—*Utility*."

His abrupt incursion into the " Queen Anne " discussion was probably due to his engagement to design houses for the middle-class people of superior taste who were to be catered for on the Bedford Park Estate—they were moderns, not mediaevals.

In an unobtrusive way Edward was altering the decorative arts, unobtrusive because so far neither Du Maurier nor Lewis F. Day had recognised his ideals or glimpsed the costumes which Ellen wore so charmingly. One small detail will serve to reveal how Godwin's suggestions are yet of effect.

At this date all artists framed their pictures in gilt frames. Edward visited an exhibition of murals by Thomas Armstrong, a painter with a liking for blue, grey and silver colour schemes, and of other works by Val Prinsep, the son of Thorby of Little

[1] *The Building News*, March 13th, 1875, p. 285.

Holland House. When he came away he wrote out his suggestions: that the pictures should be arranged at eye level in a panelled wall which should be painted in the prevailing tone of the pictures; that the mould of the panel bordering the picture ought to be gilded and afterward similarly painted, and that then some of the paint should be wiped off in order that flecks of gold should show amidst the paint.

When, two years later, Godwin's friend, James McNeill Whistler, treated his frames in the manner Edward had suggested—in blue with flecks of gold—Lewis F. Day, the decorative designer, commented: "It is cleverly done. One thing it will attract noticeably. It will be remembered as the most frantic specimen of decoration in the furniture of 1878," and continued to point out that it was "in the Anglo-Japanese style which we are beginning to associate with the name of Edward W. Godwin", yet the scumbling of frames is still practised by artists who are unconscious of its origin.

In November 1875, a writer in the *Daily News*, taking as his theme a recent speech by W. E. Gladstone—published his opinions upon the nature of Art. His outburst was greeted by Godwin with the words: "The year's twaddle about art has risen to its highest flood within the last fortnight. . . ."[1]

Some of the statements of the newspaper writer which provoked his outburst were as here quoted:

"We cannot be classic Greeks; and we could not feel to art as they did without becoming like them.

"We cannot give ourselves up as a people to the worship and culture of mere beauty.

"It is quite possible, sometimes, to combine in a wonderful degree the purposes of utility with the purposes of beauty. Any great cathedral will make this evident; so will a really artistic tea-cup."

To this Godwin retorted:

"To tell us that 'we cannot be classic Greeks' is just as futile and as unnecessary as it would be to say that we cannot be Hebrew apostles. To cease the practice of Christian virtue or the good because we cannot be Galilean fishermen and be cruci-

[1] *The Architect*, November 20th, 1875, p. 281.

fied, would be just as reasonable as to cease the practice of natural virtue or the beautiful because we cannot be Phidias, Ictinus or Apelles.

" No one wants to be a Galilean fisherman, and no one wants to be a ' classic Greek ', and yet we may well long for the virtues of both.

" Nor am I aware that any, the most visually sensitive among us, want the English people to give themselves up ' to the worship and culture of mere beauty '. The word ' mere ' in the expression ' mere beauty ' means, I suppose, much about the same as the word ' really ' in the expression ' a really artistic tea-cup '. What the difference may be between an artistic tea-cup and a really artistic one may not be so self-evident as the critic of the *Daily News* seems to think."

Although Godwin was an artist, and has been singled out by Sir Max Beerbohm as " the greatest aesthete of them all ", he never used the expressions that were attributed to the followers of the cult.

CHAPTER IX

THREE HOUSES

THE ARTISTIC success of Edward and Ellen in the production of *The Merchant of Venice* might have been expected to have had a happy issue, for each of them had proved their capacity in their separate arts. Ellen had established her reputation as a wonderful actress. He, according to Herbert Tree, had wrought a revolution in the theatrical world through the character of his settings and costume. It was natural to suppose that they would together proceed from one success to another.

But both of them were highly strung and impetuous, and what followed was least expected. In the words of Miss Terry, he "went away and shut the door after him". Someone said: "It was in a fit of pique."[1] Venus de Milo followed him, for she had no value in the broker's eyes.

The facts that have been transmitted are scanty. These are that the breach was sudden and unexpected, and that some of Ellen's advisers were urging her to leave Godwin.

If "pique" were the cause, it is possible that the information that her friends were pressing her to part from him had come to his knowledge, and that some hasty words may have provoked him to act—as he imagined—first. If reason entered into the action it may have been that Godwin knew that divorce was not to be expected so long as he remained with her. That is, that Watts had resolved that he would never facilitate their marriage. Yet even this last is insufficient excuse in cold blood, and unlikely to have been more than an afterthought.

Whatsoever the cause, in 1875 (the exact day is not known), when the breach took place, Godwin's conduct in leaving

[1] Ellen Terry, *Memoirs*, p. 97.

Ellen and his two children appeared reprehensible. She thought possibly he would return, but time passed and there was no sign from him. He had made up his mind in one of those moods that changed his life: leaving Bristol had been one; eloping with Ellen another; and now desertion. Ellen continued her stage engagements. In November she was playing in *Masks and Faces* at the Prince of Wales, one of Taylor and Reade's plays that to-day continues to give pleasure. The Press commended her acting. " A more truthful performance could be hardly imagined."[1]

She had left Taviton Street, and, with the children, gone back to Harpenden.

As for Edward, up to the turn of the year his writing continued to appear week by week in *The Architect*, concluding in December with an article headed, *The Hope of the Family*, which dwelt upon the work of the promising young sculptors in the Academy School. Living in Essex Street, Strand, he had apparently not changed his habits of visiting his club for lunch and dinner and working in the office each day, so that it must have come as a shock to those of his colleagues who had accepted his attachment for Ellen as forgivable, when they heard belatedly that he had married! The woman had tempted him.

The ceremony had taken place on January 4th, 1876, in the Strand Registry Office before the Registrar and the Superintendent Registrar, in the presence of two witnesses apparently provided by the officials for a fee. The bride was Beatrice Philip, a young lady, said to have been a pupil in her husband's office, possibly an aspirant who had been attracted by his essay upon the employment of women in the profession two years earlier.

The marriage certificate is interesting. It is made out and signed in the name of Edwin Godwin; his age is given as forty-one, and his father is described as a builder. The facts are, his Christian name was Edward William on his baptismal certificate and first marriage, and he always signed his name as Edward; his true age was forty-two, and his father's occupation differs from that on his first marriage and baptismal certificates. The probable explanation of these differences is that his second

[1] *The Graphic*, November 13th, 1875, p. 479.

wife called him Edwin, and, as mentioned earlier, that his father was connected in later life with the firm of Godwin, Smith and Co. at Bristol. The second Mrs. Godwin gave her age as twenty-one years. She was one of the younger of the several daughters of John Birnie Philip, the sculptor for Sir Gilbert Scott on the podium of the Albert Memorial, and for the same architect on that of the Foreign Office. He had died of bronchitis, suddenly, early in March 1875.

Beatrice Godwin was a brunette, handsome and French-looking, and singularly described as " large " by some and " little " by other persons who knew her, the contradiction being presumably due to the commentator contrasting the lady against his or her own stature. She was, in fact, about five feet five in height. She was a lively young lady given to hero-worship, Bohemian, and an amateur in several arts. It was as well that Beatrice was used to the society of artists, for after the wedding Edward took his bride to the combination of house and office and there left her to go and dine at his club. The scandal-mongers, when they knew, made much of this, yet it was probably designed to defer their knowledge that any change had taken place in his condition.

The subsequent relationship of the principal angles of the triangle one to another does not help in the elucidation of the mystery. It tends to suggest that, whatever the cause of their action at the time, they felt differently later. Watts confessed to Ellen that he had ruined her life and begged for forgiveness. She, until her last breath, continued to hold Edward dear, he to admire her consummate acting, and to take a pride in her career. Perhaps for all of them it had been for the best. Watts soon gave Ellen her freedom and she remarried. Much later he himself remarried.

The newly wedded Godwins visited Belgium by way of Antwerp and then proceeded up the Rhine. On their return, Edward resumed his comments on current architectural topics as if nothing had disturbed the order of his life. As an architect, he supervised the building of his several houses : the first, and most able, on the newly commenced Bedford Park Estate, and another in Billing Road, Northampton, for someone who named it Rheinfieldon. The house has some interesting touches, among them the lofty chimney stack; the construction of the dormer; the two circular turrets (of which the smaller is shown), and the corbelled balcony. It bore the impress of the Rhine holiday. The house has been spoiled by the addition, by another architect, of a porch and conservatories, and further disfigured by enemy action.

The newspapers had just discovered that there was something stirring in artistic circles. At first they were pleased to call the fashion the Nick-Nack Mania, and to condemn the followers. " A man who deliberately devotes the whole of his spare time, money and energy in filling his home with Bristol chocolate cups, original willow-pattern plates, Japanese dragons, spindle-legged tables, Chelsea shepherdesses, Dresden boys in blue coats and red knee-breeches, Stradivarius fiddles without strings, antique bellows without nozzles and enamelled snuff boxes without hinges, is—if the plain truth is to be told—a poor miserable creature."[1]

This was directed against the pre-Raphaelite Rossetti rather than the aesthetes, to whom it hardly applied. Moreover, anyone who devoted his *whole* time must have been a dealer. But by midsummer, June and July 1876, *Punch* had become interested, and published illustrated jests about " musical aesthetics ", the preliminary uncertain recognition of the altered trend of taste.

Notwithstanding the reference to Bristol chocolate cups, Godwin was more concerned about Mr. Hankey's lofty building divided into flats at Queen Anne's Gate. The mansions served him as a peg upon which to hang a treatise on the most suitable height for living rooms, for he could not understand, he explained, why the middle classes wanted rooms twelve to thirteen feet high. Then, with his usual prescience, he made the revolutionary suggestion that nine feet or eight feet six inches was quite enough. In the same article he found fault with " the foolish habit of looping window curtains instead of hanging them straight ". It was suggestions of this nature that gave Edward Godwin his reputation as an eccentric. If they had been widely heeded, Victorian furnishing would have changed in its character sooner than actually occurred.

[1]*The British Architect*, February 11th, 1876, p. 74.

He was still much impressed by Japanese and Chinese art. In his spare time he was occupied in the design of a range of house furniture that had been labelled as Anglo-Japanese by his rivals, but which might more accurately have been called simple light-made furniture, because its most noticeable characteristics were those two. But the public needed a label and Japan was as suitable to their taste as any other. In some of Godwin's furniture of this date the influence of the Victorian customer lingers in the over-plentiful provision of shelves for the support of loose ornaments (nick-nacks) that seldom had any relation to the use of the piece of furniture. Beatrice Godwin helped in the decoration of many of his designs, her contribution consisting in the painting of panels representing Spring, Summer, Autumn, Winter and the like, either as figures or flowers, birds or trees, appropriate to the season. She was a clever decorator, soon to be a pupil with James McNeill Whistler. Some of Edward's pieces of furniture were named after his young wife—Beatrice.

For at least ten years Godwin had studied Japanese principles of design. Now, in 1876, when the aesthetes were beginning to appreciate the decorative quality of Eastern prints, and the *Magazine of Art* had devoted some space to the explanation of the subject, Edward was already lamenting the decline in colour arrangements and the loss of constructional truth in the Japanese products offered for sale. He attributed this decline to the increased contact with Western civilisation and to the growing demand for Japanese goods among those who were not capable of assessing their artistic quality. Anything styled Oriental was certain to be bought, its sale pushed because the profit on the productions of rice-eating labour was exorbitant.

Twice during the year he returned, in prose, to the theme of Japanese art. In one of these articles he described how he had visited a warehouse in which the products of Japanese workmanship were housed. He found there a fellow architect, a nobleman, a baronet and a bevy of ladies waiting for a consignment of goods to arrive; when these customers were told, by an assistant, that the goods would not be delivered until the evening, they faded away.

The moral of this anecdote was that, although the building

was packed full for its several floors with all kinds of treasures, the waiting group of collectors were only anxious to buy the latest novelties. Charles Eastlake, in *Hints to Household Taste*, had reached a like conclusion, in that he attributed the decline of workmanship, European in his case, to the craze for novelty among the richer middle classes. It was something different that they required, not something worth buying for its intrinsic worth.

Although he had parted from Ellen, his theatrical undertakings were not to end. The artistic success of the Bancrofts' *Merchant of Venice* suggested to Phelps and Coleman that it would be a help if they engaged Godwin to assist them to produce *Henry V* at the Queen's Theatre. They gave Beatrice Godwin a small part. Large yellow posters (an unconscious anticipation of the coming fervour for this colour), announcing that E. W. Godwin was responsible for the decor and costume, were pasted on the hoardings.

In advance of the first performance, Godwin published a long account of the research he had made before advising on the play's production. Friend William Burges read one of the posters, and though he was rather disturbed by their vivid colour, and notwithstanding his foreboding that they spelt no good, he not altogether surprisingly went to see the performance. He then noticed some solecisms to which he hastened to draw attention in print, in a critical review which was promptly answered in another article by Godwin, who claimed that the errors had been imported into the play by Coleman, who had been over-persuaded by some of his friends. As promptly William Burges retorted that in that case Edward should, for his own reputation, insist that his name be taken off the poster! From Harpenden Ellen could feel amused. The biter had been bitten.

Possibly Burges' advice was good, for, from what we know of Godwin, if he had felt that there was any misrepresentation he would have resigned. The alterations suggested, however, do not appear to have been sufficiently serious to warrant that course. Moreover, it is not impossible that the intervention of Burges was an elaborate rebuke at the expense of his friend, for his article was in the manner of his victim who was prone to dot the i's and cross the t's of other people. Anyway it provided Godwin with something to think about. Naturally the dispute gave a fillip to the attendances, for when doctors disagree the patient's friends decide. Burges had sugared the pill by referring to his opponent as " an excellent architect ".

Burges had, himself, recently been the centre of the controversy about the decoration of St. Paul's, of which he had been appointed " architect for the completion ", and was not feeling pleased with life. More to his liking, he was working on the sketch designs of a house for his own occupation in Melbury Road, which was to illustrate his amalgam of Greek and Gothic motifs.

Although he had now added theatrical production to his other activities, Godwin yet had time for architecture. He was as successful as ever, gaining this year, 1877, the first premium for a chapel for the Nottingham Church Cemetery Company, a small building, and for some swimming baths in Manchester. The greater part of his work, however, consisted of the design of several houses for artists. Some of the clients were introduced to him by Whistler, the remainder being either acquaintances of his wife, the daughter of a sculptor they had met in her childhood, or members of the Hogarth or Art Club.

For how long he had known Whistler is uncertain. They were friends at the time of his sojourn with Ellen at Harpenden, when the artist and the Art Club were no doubt in part responsible for his late nights. He had most probably met him before he removed from Bristol, for he was familiar with Whistler's first London studio. After his second marriage their association became very close. In this admiration Beatrice Godwin joined. She was a clever young woman, ambitious to become a painter of more than cabinets. To help her further her aim, Whistler gave her some lessons, permitting her to watch him at work. They were mutually attracted—Beatrice being fascinated by the American and he drawn to her.

The artist's taste in decoration was curiously similar to that which Godwin had favoured so long for his own houses. His drawing-room was nearly empty, only a large sofa, two or three chairs and a Chippendale table served as furniture, and the floor

was covered with pale, straw-coloured matting. Such a setting
might have been Edward's. Indeed they subsequently collaborated so frequently, so many times, in decorative schemes,
that it is hardly possible to attribute with certainty their respective contributions to the whole. The idea was frequently
Edward's when the execution was undoubtedly Whistler's.
At every possible opportunity, in public and private, Godwin
espoused the cause of his friend; he was very early in recognising
his genius as an etcher, being his first and only advocate. Known
to but few in these early days, James was not so difficult a man to
befriend as he afterwards became. His notoriety was hidden in
the near future.

In 1877 Sir Coutts Lindsay, his wife, C. E. Hallé and Comyns
Carr, to give the artists of unorthodox expression the opportunity
to make their work known more widely, opened the Grosvenor
Gallery. It was built from the designs by William Sam, on a
plot of land leased from the Duke of Westminster between Brook
Street and Grosvenor Street. The hanging area was about half
that of the Royal Academy, to which Sir Coutts made it plain
that the new gallery was not antagonistic. Still, he invited only
those artists to contribute whose works he wanted to show.
Among the invited on the first occasion were Rossetti, Burne-
Jones, Whistler, Albert Moore and Louise Jopling.

D. G. Rossetti declined. Burne-Jones lent his water colours,
Fides and *Spes*, and the six panels of the *Angels of Creation*, the
Beguiling of Merlin and *The Mirror of Venus*. Whistler lent some
of his nocturnes. The galleries were furnished with selected
antiques, and the pictures were hung with care, well spaced with
respect for each other, so that they might appear to the best advantage. The walls were draped with a faded red damask, the
ceiling blue with stars of silver. The red background was undoubtedly a mistake. Ruskin said, after seeing the show, " that
he found the furnishing grievously injurious to the best pictures ".
His best were those of Burne-Jones.

The occasion of the opening of the Gallery was a much
publicised event. The Prince and Princess of Wales signified
that they would attend, and if the Prince favoured anything the
rest of society were sure to follow his example. At the private

view, Royalty and the select were entertained to dinner in the restaurant below the Gallery. Afterwards a reception followed in the Galleries upstairs for them and for the crush who could not be accommodated at dinner. All the elegant were there.

It was the drawing of Burne-Jones that caused the most excitement. There were amid the throng several ladies coiffed like his paintings and having faces and figures little different from the mythical creatures he had visualised, Beatrice Godwin among them. Thereafter the ultra-fashionable adopted a similar pose. The conventional philistines smiled.

Among those who were much interested was the young Oscar Wilde. He was quick to contribute a long account of the show to *The Dublin University Magazine.* John Ruskin went away to write his views for publication in *Fors Clavigera.*

The Whistler pictures could not compete with the works of Burne-Jones in popular appeal. They lacked human interest. You can claim to understand a nocturne, but you cannot easily dress as one. Whistler's nocturnes, "the tender blue of twilight seen through the windows of a lamp-lit room", puzzled the gathering, as pictures with any claim to originality always have done.

You can, however, make a jest of their kind, and this was soon done. At the Gaiety Theatre the author of a burlesque called *The Grasshopper* welcomed the opportunity. A counterfeit of Whistler's landscape manner was shown on the stage, one way up as *A Sunset at Sea* while reversed the same served as *A Desert Scene.* Twenty years after, this performance was a stock pantomime antic. In *The Grasshopper* characters representing Whistler, Wilde and Frank Miles had a song and dance. It was to be some years before Max Nordau could say of Whistler: "The woman of a given epoch likes to form herself on the ideal which the art and poetry of the time give of the 'interesting' woman. Thus Whistler, by means of his female portraits, became an educator of the aesthetically superfine women of the present day."[1]

The opening of the Grosvenor Gallery, by reason of the notice that it drew, made it difficult for anyone to ignore the new tendencies. Many things that had seemed ridiculous now became

[1]*On Art and Artists,* Max Nordau, 1906, p. 154.

fashionable. In the small circles of the cultivated Godwin could
now move as an exponent of correct taste. He was not now crying
solitary in the wilderness.

None the less, the architectural example of the exquisite was
still awaited, and this Whistler, Edward and his wife were nightly
in conspiracy to create. Whistler had secured a site in Tite
Street, adjoining the western boundary of Chelsea Hospital,
and upon it he planned to build an ideal house. The building
was to include a studio, a school for pupils, and a residence for
the artist owner. The top floor was to hold a large studio
forty-seven feet by thirty, a drawing-room studio thirty by
twenty ; five bedrooms, a dining-room and kitchen, and all the
usual offices, completed the accommodation in the house. It was
but small. The exterior was to be Edward's interpretation of
modern architecture carried out in white brick capped by a green
roof. Both Whistler and he were entranced in anticipation by the
colour scheme. In architectural circles the building was rumoured
to be " one of the surprises of next season ". It was to be as plain
as a pikestaff. Such relief or mouldings as were used were derived
from Grecian precedents. The interior was to be as novel as the
exterior, with mantelpieces that were to be distinct and entirely
original varieties of that important feature. The stage was being
set for an architectural revolution. There was not another
architect in the world who could have satisfied Whistler.

Whilst the plotting was afoot, the two schemers were col-
laborating in the design of a room and furniture to be made by
Watt and shown at the Paris Exhibition, for which Whistler
had arranged to paint the wall decorations. The room was to
be a try-out for the interior of his own house and an indication
of the world to come.

Not far away from the site of the White House, as it was named
with double intention, on land one time part of the Little Holland
House garden, William Burges was now constructing a Greek
Gothic residence for his own occupation. The relationship of
the two—Greek and Gothic—had been the subject of a lecture
by him at the recent Conference of Architects. In his lecture he
had found kinship between Herodotus and Froissart, Aristo-
phanes and Rabelais—a notion he had held ever since he and

Godwin had met in Buckingham Street. For the Queen Anne style—once called by him " negro art "—he had no use, " its practitioners are deserters from the Gothic field, due to the work of Thackeray ", which, indeed, was undoubtedly in part true. He also wondered aloud if the Queen Anne would be preserved in the future as beautiful. The lecture must have been more impressive than any of the reports of it, because it was referred to frequently, by architects who had heard it, long after it had been delivered.

The two houses were in marked contrast. Moreover, they show how over the years the two architects, who in their early days had held similar views on the main elements of architecture, had diverged from this agreement. The White House was to be as fresh in conception as the designer could make it. Melbury Road, as Burges' house was called, was to be an amalgam of mediaeval and Grecian motifs, ornate both in its structural features and its movable furnishings. These last had been made from drawings by Burges over a number of years ; the earlier had been decorated by Simeon Solomon, Burne-Jones and other painters, then as young as he, but now in turn dead or prominent and celebrated. When the two houses were sufficiently advanced toward completion to debate about, they were discussed by critics in England and America. Most of the writers said that they pre- ferred that by Burges, which they pronounced rational and pleasing, while the White House was generally condemned as strange and a disfigurement. The fact is, they could not be compared ; the one was archaeology with a dash of modernity, the other modern with the fewest possible concessions to past periods and those imposed by the authorities.

The disapproval with which they were greeted was no new experience for Whistler or his architect. They retorted : " The architect has placed his windows and door where they are wanted, and not with Baker Street regularity ", the last few words being intended to protect them from the charge that " Queen Anne led to Harley Street ", the first words to emphasise the Gothic nature of their functional conception.

Fortunately for Godwin, there were friends of his and Whistler's who had enough perception to admire the novel house, and

A. K. Bray. del.

THE WHITE HOUSE, CHELSEA.
Reconstruction as approved. 1878.

sufficient courage and cash to support the architect in a practical
way by employing him to design for them not dissimilar houses.
Young Archie Stuart Wortley was one of them. He had bought
three plots of ground adjoining the White House. On this land
he instructed Edward to design him a larger house than his
neighbour. Frank Miles, well known for his pencil drawings of
female heads, notably of little Connie Gilchrist, commissioned
another. The house for Miles was that upon which he bestowed
most thought. It contained nine rooms and a studio forty feet
long at the top of the house. Miles was a bachelor who afterwards
mysteriously went crazy. Godwin said of the house for Miles :

> " When the first elevation was sent to the Board of Works
> our respected friend, Mr. Vulliamy, said, 'Why, this is worse
> than Whistler's', that it would be useless to lay it before the
> Board, and that it would not do, and yet I consider it the best
> thing I ever did. I grant you there was no cornice, no parapet
> and no string course. But is architecture a matter of string
> courses and parapets. . . . Because I choose to do something
> different to the conventional, because I was not in fashion,
> and because the Board and its officers knew nothing by
> experience of the nature of my work, the Board refused to let
> my design be carried out.
>
> " Well, I made a second design, in which I introduced a
> number of reminiscences of a visit to Holland, and the thing
> was pronounced charming. This is very sad.
>
> " I am bold enough to say I am a better judge than the
> Board of Works as to what is right in architecture. There is
> no chance for art or originality when such things as that go on
> at Spring Gardens."[1]

That was why the house of Frank Miles was not the work
of art it might have been. When the client did not spoil the
design, the local authority did the damage on his behalf.

Others who engaged him were Rosa Corder, the animal painter
and friend of Charles Augustus Howell; Slingsby Bethell and
C. Pellegrini, the cartoonist APE of *Vanity Fair*, who had

[1] E. W. G., *The Building News*, March 7th, 1879, p. 261.

arrived in London penniless and now liked to show his friends the doorstep on which he had slept. All these became his clients, and for them he designed studio homes. Finally, the Princess Louise, herself an artist, graciously commissioned him to design for her a small barnlike studio in Kensington Gardens.

Miss Rosa Corder's was a picturesque little cottage. Several of the Tite Street studios form a group, although it is obvious that they were commissioned from time to time and that the different demands of the owners had made it impossible to combine individually pleasing houses into a satisfactory composition. To make this more difficult, a house by R. W. Edis is the link between two of Godwin's. Despite his outstanding skill in asymmetrical arrangement, the result was unfortunate.

While he and Beatrice spent hours with Whistler discussing the details of his house they listened to the master's denunciation of his brother-in-law, Seymour Haden, who had sinned beyond pardon when he had added the legs of his daughter Annie to the plate that James had etched. They listened, also, to their friend's plans for the discomfiture of John Ruskin whom he was pursuing for libel over his opinion of one of the Grosvenor Gallery nocturnes, in *Fors Clavigera*.

It was October before the White House was at last sufficiently finished for occupation. The delighted owner staged a house-warming when a private view was had of his coming exhibits for the second exhibition at the Grosvenor Gallery. All his admirers, friends and neighbour artists were there. One of them, the lithographer T. R. Way, set down this memory of the occasion. " I remember a long, not very lofty room, very light, with windows along one side. . . . The pictures shown were Connie Gilchrist skipping. Three girls—and in the drawing-room below the *Rosa Corder*." The subject was the lady artist for whom Godwin had planned her little cottage. The picture represented her as " a fair woman, in a black jacket and long black skirt, standing in profile against a black background, holding in her right hand a plumed hat ". The pose was one that she had taken unconsciously and that Whistler had glimpsed and asked her to repeat. Miss Corder and Howell, Edward and his wife, Archie Wortley and all the rest, the friends he could afford, were there. The only shadow on the blind was that of Ruskin. Howell, like Whistler, had a lawsuit pending, and for this he had enlisted Godwin as a professional witness. As the architect for the White House and an outright admirer of the artist's work, he could not be much use in the Whistler libel action.

The first of the two *causes célebrès*, that of Whistler and Ruskin, came before Baron Huddleston and a special jury on November 15th. The claimant asked for £1,000 damages, the provocation alleged being the extraordinary words written by the critic following his tour of the Grosvenor Gallery Exhibition: " I have seen and heard much of cockney impudence before now, but never expected to hear a coxcomb ask two hundred guineas for flinging a pot of paint in the public's face."

The painting which had excited Ruskin's ire was called by the artist *Nocturne in Black and Gold—The Falling Rocket*. The offending Ruskin was unable to attend the hearing as he had had an attack of brain fever and his place as chief witness for the defence was reluctantly taken by Burne-Jones. As a fellow exhibitor at the Grosvenor Gallery, he might be expected to have examined his colleague's works, or, if not, to have studied them at the private view arranged by Whistler for the benefit of any witnesses.

In the serious atmosphere of a Court of Law, little wit is needed to cause lots of laughter. The offending picture was shown in court as evidence for the defence. Light amusement was caused when counsel disputed as to which was the right way up.

ATTORNEY-GENERAL (for Ruskin): " You are holding it upside down."

SERGEANT PARRY (for plaintiff): " No I'm not."

SIR JOHN HOLKER, Attorney-General: " I tell you, you are."

When Burne-Jones entered the box he testified that the picture was more like a sketch than a finished picture. He admitted, however, that it had colour and atmosphere, but it lacked detail. This was the pre-Raphaelite dogma of fidelity to nature which Burne-Jones had one time held through acquaintance with Rossetti.

The next witness, W. P. Frith, R.A., said that in his opinion Whistler's pictures " were not serious works of art ". He was never likely to have admired any picture by Whistler, for he was an artist of crowds, each figure in which was recognisable as in his *Derby Day, Paddington Station* or other elaborate social documents. At the R.A. his compositions were so popular that they had to be railed from the crowd.

Tom Taylor, Poor Law Commissioner, Editor of *Punch* and friend of Ellen, followed. He took from his pockets clippings from *The Times*, read nervously what he had written of the plaintiff's paintings, which, by the way, were quite fair comment. He was a poor witness, contributing very little to clarify the points in dispute.

The plaintiff, Whistler, under cross-examination by the Attorney-General, was asked how long it had taken him to " knock it off ". He replied : " Two days at a rough estimate."

The Attorney-General countered : " Two hundred guineas was not excessive for two days' work ? "

" No, I ask it for the knowledge of a lifetime."

Following a patient hearing, the jury returned a verdict in favour of Whistler. It could hardly have been otherwise. The damage was assessed at one farthing. When the whole episode was over and forgotten, he wore the coin on his watch-chain. Ruskin's costs amounted to £352 12s. 4d. and were paid by his friends. The journal *L'Art* opened a subscription list for Whistler, but little money was subscribed to it.

Edward was one of the spectators at the trial, and like the rest of Whistler's admirers, he was disappointed with the verdict. He expressed the opinion that the damages were absurd, and " that the language was defamatory and libellous, the judge over and over again declared, and the question left to the jury was whether the words used by Mr. Ruskin were written as a fair and *bona fide* expression of opinion on—and mark this—the work of Mr. Whistler. If they referred to Mr. Whistler and not to his work, they were not privileged ". Ruskin, a popular figure, had at the time of the libel only recently recovered from a breakdown, and before the trial he had had another. The jury appear, on this account, to have reduced the damages, and certainly the punishment hardly fitted the crime. The case did nobody, save the lawyers, any good. For the moment it embarrassed Whistler, and it ruined Godwin's White House design for ever.

A week later the second lawsuit was staged. This time it was not a picture which was the subject of dispute, but a house—a genuine Queen Anne mansion—Chaldon House. Furthermore, to those familiar with the plaintiff in the case, it promised to be amusing. The dispute was over the amount of compensation which the Metropolitan District Railway should pay Charles Augustus Howell for the loss of the use of Chaldon House, Fulham—a Queen Anne house of which he held the lease, and upon which he said he had expended at least seventeen hundred pounds in order to adapt it as his place of business as a dealer in works of art, antique and modern.

Howell was a curious and mysterious character. At one time he had been John Ruskin's secretary, and afterwards amusingly claimed " to have written Ruskin's books for him ", which, in his clerical capacity, may have been true. He had been Rossetti's right-hand man, the vendor of his pictures and the agent who had recovered the poet's manuscript poems from his wife's grave. Now he was acting for Whistler and dealing in anything the artist would allow him to handle or, without permission, such things as he could lay hand upon. While his methods were quite unorthodox, Howell had been on the whole a useful agent for the artists. Although he helped himself, he certainly helped them, and, since they were both unbusinesslike, the methods he employed to recoup himself for his services saved them and him a lot of anxiety. There were few people he did not know. Some of them thought wryly that they knew Howell.

Edward was called as a witness in the case. Three days before the hearing, in order to have his recollection of the place fresh in his memory when he gave his evidence, he visited Chaldon House, accompanied by Pellegrini. When they arrived they found Howell engaged in weeding the path up to the front door. He left no stone unturned.

The pleas were heard in the Sheriff's Court, Red Lion Square, on November 27th, 1878, the court being filled by as many artists and aesthetes as could crowd in. Most of them had attended the Whistler case, and nobody wanted to miss the fun, for, when Howell was concerned, anything might happen. Besides, it was, like the picture trial had been, a form of contest for the kind of art for which they professed regard.

Mr. Grantham, Q.C., M.P., and Horace Brown were for Howell, Mr. Bidder, Q.C., and Mr. Bickersteth for the Company.

The plaintiff entered the box and described himself as being a D.C.L., Civil Engineer and a member of many scientific bodies in England and abroad, and as having dealt in art for twelve years. Chaldon House, he said, was of a unique character, although, when he first saw it, it was the wreck of a fine house. He had leased it for twenty-one years and had covenanted to spend £500 on repairs, his actual expenses being £2,000, of which £1,700 could be proved. The rooms were decorated with Morris papers costing 14s. and 15s. a piece, and he had fitted several mantelpieces. The place, he claimed, had grown into an artist's paradise, particularly adapted to his profession, for he could " fill a room with drawings by Rossetti one day and with pictures by Titian the next ".

Then he continued : " My connection in the art world is very considerable. I am known as a collector of works of art. If people are in the collecting humour they will buy, and if they are not in that humour I soon put them in it. (*Laughter.*) Mine is a genuine Queen Anne house. I know the collections of most connoisseurs. People come to the house because they like me, and because I make them comfortable. (*Laughter.*) When I lived at North End they came to see me there. If I lived anywhere else they will come in the same way. . . . I buy Whistler's pictures at his house. I take them home and hang them up and I never laugh, I never even smile. A man comes who appreciates a nocturne, and he goes mad till he gets that particular one. I cannot allow a friend to remain in that critical state and then he gets it."

At this moment Whistler, small and dapper, entered the court. Howell waved his welcome. " An arrangement in black and white," he exclaimed.

Mr. Bidder, Q.C., asked a number of questions, but failed to shake the witness. Then, having mentioned Whistler's arrangements, he asked :

"I suppose the green is the customer and the gold the money they bring?"

"No. The gold is thrown in to show there is no ill-feeling."

The principal professional witness for Howell was Godwin, who gave his address as Victoria Chambers, Westminster.

After having told the court how long he had been acquainted with Howell and his house, he explained that he had known him when he lived at Northolt. Then, referring to Chaldon House, he continued : " The house was a house alone. I should think that it would let at £400 a year at the least." He could not account for its being let at £120. It was a mystery. " I cannot explain why it did not fetch £2,200 when it was put up for auction. It was curious, as curious as some of the things I saw in the house."

" Do you think that it is possible to get subscribers to a portrait of Thomas Carlyle in a common house ? " asked Mr. Bidder, alluding to reproductions of Whistler's *Carlyle* which Howell was selling.

"It depends on the character of the house, and the social position of the owner."

" Can a nocturne in black and gold be only dealt with in a Queen Anne house ? "

" I do not know how people deal in nocturnes."[1]

That concluded his evidence. More witnesses gave conflicting testimony as to the value of the place. The case was very half-heartedly contested by the Company and eventually judgement was given for Howell for £3,650. The claimant appeared content, clean-shaven and green-complexioned; he lit a cigarette and, with Miss Corder and his supporters, left the court.

The following day Edward went north. He had an appointment to speak to the Manchester Society of Architects.

[1] *The Building News*, 1879, Vol. XXXVI, p. 261.

Chapter X

THE AESTHETES

O N HIS return to town, after his visit to Manchester when he had told how his childhood environment had influenced his life, and given an outline of the latter, he was asked, as the designer of the notorious White House, to lecture to the Architectural Association. The house was the subject of first interest to the profession, the younger members of which regarded it as the most promising example of the possibility of a breach with the style-ridden architecture of the past.

He readily agreed. His original intention had been to talk about what he called " trimmings ", a title chosen because the authorities had insisted that ornamental panels be added to the elevations of the perfectly plain White House and to the even plainer studio of Frank Miles.

However, when, on an evening in March, he arrived in Conduit Street to keep his promise, he had to confess : " Gentlemen, I stand here in a very awkward predicament. I have lost my lecture. Where, I have not the slightest conception. Up to ten o'clock last night it was safe and written, and between that hour and ten this morning it disappeared. This morning I saw your secretary, and said: ' I shall back out of it. I have written my lecture as promised, and now it is gone, there's an end of it.' Mr. Page said : ' No, you are the thing we want, and not the lecture.' Well, I am here simply to talk about a few studios. I shall divide my sermon into three heads. (I am, you see, quite orthodox and regular.) First, detached studios ; second, studios in groups ; third, studios in houses—converted stables." He was an attractive extemporary speaker.

His audience was not disappointed. He was very popular with the student members of the Architectural Association, not only because of the help he was always ready to give them, but by reason of their realisation of his gifts. Since he had designed so many studios he was regarded as a specialist, indeed his only competitor in this type of building design was R. Norman Shaw, whose work suited the less adventurous members of the Royal Academy. Most of Shaw's studios were Elizabethan period pieces rather than artists' workshops, whereas until they were built nobody had ever seen anything like those emanating from Godwin's brain. Their interiors are remarkable for their beauty and the fittings for their suitability. Their exteriors had to conform with the Board's opinions.

Having made his explanation, he continued in his familiar intimate manner :

" The artist is the most extraordinary client that you can deal with—every individual painter has his individual idea as to what a studio should be. One tells me that he wants the light to come straight down from the roof. Another says he must only have a window light. While Pellegrini declares he will have nothing but light—walls and roofs, all must give light. One would be driven mad if he had many artists as clients."

Then he turned to the main theme : " On the wall are a series of plans and designs relating to a house I have carried out for my old friend Mr. Whistler." The audience applauded the name of the artist. " He used to paint in one of the ordinary first-floor rooms looking on the British Museum. Whistler moved to Chelsea, to a very different house in Cheyne Walk, built by Sir Christopher Wren ; a small studio with black oak panelling, looking nearly west and with a light somewhat vague and foggy —just the terms in which the Attorney-General was pleased to describe his pictures the other day. I thought he was working under studio disadvantages, and on my suggestion he took two plots of ground in Tite Street, which at the back looked north-ward over Chelsea Hospital grounds."

He continued to tell his audience how the Metropolitan Board of Works did not like the original design for the house. " They said it was like a dead house." That was because it was devoid of all ornament or " trimmings ". When asked if they had any other objection, "they added, it is all roof". The reason for this was "that to put as much useful space as possible in the roof was the most economical way of building". To counter this objection he produced a perspective to show that the roof would not show to the extent they imagined. When the Board saw this they exclaimed: "We judge by the elevation." After a lot of argument, the Board gave permission to build the house, on condition that some decorative panels were added to the elevation. The panels were added, but the carving of them was never done, for it had been Whistler's intention to remove the panels when the Board had had time to forget. The staircase was spiral. Someone asked Godwin: "What kind of blinds are most suitable for an artist's studio?" "Whistler," he replied, "always used white blinds as they did not tinge the studio with any distracting tinted light." In fact he used white muslin curtains to take the edge off the shadows.

Unluckily Whistler's term of residence in his own house was to be very brief. The costs of the Ruskin case, added to his debts and the contractors' extra accounts, made it necessary to raise money somehow. The Pennells in the *Whistler Journal* blamed Godwin. They say: "Godwin had a way of always making his estimates lower than the actual expenses and then siding entirely with the builders in case of disagreement and misunderstanding." As will be realised later, their complaint is not supported by subsequent events. Whistler was the most unforgiving of men, yet the two remained fast friends, and when he had re-established himself he turned once more to Edward for the design of a new house. Actually Whistler's loss over the house was small, if indeed he or his creditors lost anything by the sale.

When it was known that he was in difficulties—the attempt to persuade his admirers to help him adequately having failed —Howell, always resourceful, did all he could to raise the wind. He generously lent him some of his award damages, not, at the time of the loan, paid by the Railway Company, and finally, when he realised that a composition was impossible, he used all his wit to save Whistler's assets, movable prints and pictures. The newspapers made fun of the situation:

> " *Of the various arrangements we've had an array.*
> *Black and white, gold and silver, tawny and grey ;*
> *But of all the arrangements there yet remains one,*
> *And that's to arrange with the troublesome dun.*"

The last arrangement was contrived by the sale of the much abused building and such of his prints and pictures as Howell had ignored. Leyland, the chief creditor, Howell and Thomas Way, the experts, formed the committee of creditors.

On the Sunday before he left, Whistler held his last reception, Edward being amongst the guests, after which the artist climbed a ladder and wrote over the Portland stone door : " Except the Lord build the house, they labour in vain that build it. E. W. Godwin, F.S.A., built this one."

Next day he set out for Venice, commissioned by the Fine Art Society at the suggestion of their new manager, Ernest Brown.

In his absence on September 18th, 1879, the White House was bought at auction by Harry Quilter, a collector art critic of views very different from those of Whistler. He paid £2,700 for the house. Whistler was furious, Godwin disappointed, and both of them were annoyed when the new owner altered the building. Whistler, for his part, never forgave Quilter and jeered at him for years in public and private. He wrote to the *World* protesting against his vandalism in altering so exquisite a dwelling —" history," he proclaimed, " is wiped from the face of Chelsea. Where is Ruskin ? And what do Morris and Sir William Drake ? " —suggesting thus that the preservation of the house should be sponsored by the Anti-Scape Society founded by William Morris. He, at any rate, did not undervalue the work of Edward Godwin.

Quilter was a most unsuitable owner, for his ideals and ideas were devoid of all sensibility. His alterations spoiled the building. Some years later he had a book *Setentiae Artis* published in which his thoughts on art were set out, one of the more reasonable of these being : " Few of us understand what it is that we mean by Art." What followed confirmed his opinions. " In Gainsborough he sees ' a plainness almost amounting to brutality ' while

' vulgarity and snobbishness ' are the chief qualities he finds in Sir Joshua Reynolds."[1]

The damage to the market of Whistler's painting had been greater, following the libel by Ruskin, than the jury can have anticipated. One of his pictures, *The Symphony in Blue and White*, that had been bought from him for two hundred guineas, only fetched £12 10s. when it was auctioned in Glasgow soon after the lawsuit.

The abstract names by which many of Whistler's pictures were catalogued were one of the protests of the aesthetes against the tale-telling academic picture. They were used to emphasise the unimportance of the subject in a work of art. The use of musical terms to classify his arrangements in colour was a further attempt to convince the spectator of the truth of the belief in the common grammar of the arts. Whistler painted his subjects for the sensory pleasure afforded by their colour and form in composition, not as reproductions of any natural group or subject. His portraits were arrangements having little regard for the sitters' habitual environment.

His outlook was entirely different from that of the pre-Raphaelites whom Ruskin had praised for their attention to detail. They were careless about the colour scheme—truth to nature was their objective. Holman Hunt's *The Shadow of the Cross* has the hues of the rainbow in disorder.

Even when Whistler depicted buildings, as he did in Venice and London, it was as incomplete suggestion, leaving to the mind of the beholder the realisation of grace, power, height, or of those feelings that he had experienced by the contemplation of a bridge, a mysterious doorway or a candle factory.

In the realm of architecture Godwin had sought the same end. Even in his youthful days, when he had employed the language of the Middle Ages, it had been his constant endeavour to evoke emotion through his employment of mass, light, line, by arrangements as abstract as the utilitarian nature of the art admitted. They were both symbolists in their own spheres : Whistler a painter Verlaine ; Godwin an architectural Villiers de l'Isle-Adam.

---

[1] Oscar Wilde, *Pall Mall Gazette*, November 18th, 1886.

Some months before Whistler had become the occupant of the White House, he and Godwin had been looked up by their distant admirer, Oscar Wilde. He had now finished his University course with distinction and had come to London armed with introductions and anxious to attract attention to his person in the wider world. To Whistler he made himself known as an admirer; to Edward as a fellow aesthete, moreover, as the son of Sir William Wilde, the oculist-archaeologist, with his strong Irish interests.

Young Wilde was tall and impressive, slender in build, given to enthusiasm for the lily, the costumes of the past, the artistic gospel of Ruskin, and the writing of Walter Pater. Obviously he was in an involved state of mind. It was some years before he formulated a distinct philosophy of aestheticism. Wilde was to be a few years older before he lost his youthful figure, and many more before he lost his character.

In 1878, though immature, he had attained much notoriety. " I," said Louise Jopling, when she first met him, " was struck with the fineness of his intellectual brow; the way the fair hair, worn rather longer than the then fashion, waved from his forehead; and his well-cut, slightly aquiline nose."[1]

He had been one of the few who had helped John Ruskin to make the road up over Hinksey Marches. He had already been caricatured contemplating a lily as " Too Utter ", and it was rumoured that it was his habit to sit in his rooms at Oxford dressed in a plum-coloured velvet costume disguised as Prince Rupert. Nothing very serious, to be sure, but behaviour sufficiently unusual as to make people talk. He was, on the whole, a rather embarrassing follower.

Arrived in town, from his rooms in the Adelphi, he perambulated Piccadilly dressed in a peculiar costume, consisting of a loose shirt with a Byron collar, a large knotted green tie, knee breeches, silk stockings and a velvet beret. It is a fact that plenty of others have since worn very similar clothing; Paris had hundreds of young men so dressed after the first great war, but in the 'seventies Wilde was alone and consequently conspicuous. The costume drew attention to him, and advertised a phase of the movement that he had taken under his wing. For

[1] Louise Jopling, *Twenty Years of My Life*, p. 78.

any host who needed explanation, his witty conversation excused his reputed costume. He laughed away his folly—if it were folly, or needed laughing away—for there is little evidence that the incident in Piccadilly was more than an accident.

Mentally Wilde was hesitating between the ideas of Ruskin and Pater. He never succeeded in resolving the philosophy of the two into one, nor of persistently developing either. His adult ideas were a form in hedonism, but toward the end of his life he reverted to his early eclecticism. At the time he met Godwin he confused the Queen Anne and the aesthetic idea, but that was excusable, for they were then intertwined, and professed experts on decoration, like Mrs. Haweis, used the terms as interchangeable; some other writers added a third fashion, Elizabethan (they called it Early English), and dubbed it also as aesthetic.

When Wilde was in the company of Godwin or Whistler he was an attentive listener, contributing now and then an amusing epigram to the talk. When he was in society all that mattered was that he should stress the unity of the arts, talk about them knowingly, tell fascinating stories and entertain. His hosts knew less than he, and if he confused what he had heard from the expert, they were incapable of detection. Wilde was not wealthy and could not afford the company he enjoyed. It was his charm on which he traded, scattering his bread on drifting waters.

The enthusiasm for things of Japanese origin probably owed as much to Whistler as to Godwin. The artist's arrangements were the result of his study of Japanese prints and afforded a visual advertisement for the craze.

Godwin's share extended to the study of the principles employed in their design. He examined the construction of lanterns, umbrellas, boxes, furniture and houses. He had used Japanese prints as wall-decoration first of all people in England. Under his guidance Liberty's had recently been induced to deal in the products of the East. The Hon. Mrs. Brassey of Heythorp took his advice and decorated her house à la Japan, if only temporarily, for a fancy-dress ball. The notion was voted a charming innovation. While the Japanese craze had, for lots of people, the additional appeal of cheapness, it was too soon made ridiculous by those who believed Mrs. Haweis in earnest : " Fire ornaments are quite gone out, you must stick a Japanese parasol in the stove."

In effect, the liking for light Japanese products encouraged the demand for the more delicate furniture which Godwin was designing for William Watt. Bamboo settees were elegant and not uncomfortable.

The average London house was drab and dingy largely owing to the furniture, hangings and wallpapers most generally used. The value of land had made gardens a curiosity. In these circumstances the conservatory had become an extension of the room, a form of enlarged window box. In an attempt to improve the design of this adjunct, Godwin, with his assistant M. B. Adams, jointly produced a book on conservatories, a copy of which they gave to the Architectural Association. The receipt of their gift was acknowledged as " On Asiatic Conservatories " when the real title was *Artistic Conservatories*. The error was, maybe, excusable, or the misprint suitable, for Godwin was coupled in the mind of the profession with Eastern influences, and some of these glass-houses had a vaguely Oriental appearance. For their period they were an advance, but to modern eyes they look woody and amusing.

As serious architecture he had made the drawings for a large residential club—the Lancaster Club—and some houses on the Embankment. There is some doubt whether the club was ever erected. Its elevations were of French Renaissance type similar to the buildings round about L'Étoile.

At this period Godwin was more eclectic in his manners than at any other time in his career. The probable explanation is that he had to gratify the whims of his clients, potential and actual. Though the mediaeval manner was almost *démodé*, the Queen Anne was not yet firmly enthroned, nor was the modern idiom he was striving to create understood by the public, or permitted by the authorities.

The most recent competition for which he had entered was for the oratory at Brompton. Perforce this had been upon a basilican plan with an Italianate exterior. While the whole of his design is very able, the component parts of the elevation do not impress

INTERIOR DECORATIONS.

From *The British Architect*, July, 1881.

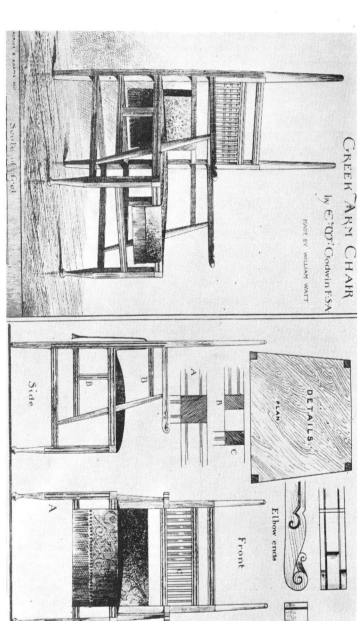

GREEK ARM CHAIR
by E. W. Godwin F.S.A.

MADE BY WILLIAM WATT

GREEK ARM CHAIR.

From *The Building News*, May, 1885.

one as entirely fused or reconciled. This is most evident in the Campanile, which seems alien to the composition.

The oratory, a much larger building, is not equal to the mortuary chapel designed by him at about the same date—or to the flats built by him for Gillow.

How he contrived to find any time to engage in the trivial social activities of his wife's choosing is a mystery, particularly when the amount of labour put into the drawings for these buildings is assessed, and when his time spent in literary work, design of costumes, wallpapers, fabrics and furniture is added. Yet he did. With his young wife he was to be seen everywhere. True, some of these engagements combined profession with pleasure. The Grosvenor Gallery afforded this duplication. At the Gallery he could meet all his friends, see and be seen— while at the same time viewing *The Golden Stairs* by Burne-Jones; *Mrs. Jopling* by Millais, or *William Morris* by Watts, and then go away and write about it all, or attend the Academy Soirée where " the dresses were of course very eccentric, and it was amusing to see how fashionable ladies tried to dress or rather to drape like artists' models and few models like fashionable ladies ". Other of his engagements were of the sort that any architect has to fulfil. In June he attended the *conversazione* at the Mansion House. The Lord Mayor's first plan had been to give three entertainments—to art, law and science—on separate evenings. Actually he welcomed all three at an overcrowded, overheated assembly, in June, where Sir Francis Wyatt Truscott, Lord Mayor, and his lady received the guests. In the 'eighties *conversaziones* were a craze. An exhibition in an ante-room invariably formed part of the scheme to entertain the assembly. Here could be enjoyed the latest novelty in electric shocks, light, telephone or telegraph. On this occasion it was the collection of plate, charters and similar treasures of the Corporation which were displayed in all manner of awkward places. Edward complained that the posteriors of the stooping visitors peering into the cases obstructed the movement of the less curious about the Mansion House. The guests, fine art, law and science were summed up. For the law he had no use—the Whistler verdict still rankled. For science, well, " the disciples of science gathered in gloomy knots and were as usual wholly indifferent to everyone else ".

Painting was represented by the P.R.A. (Leighton—" like an elderly Adonis "), Millais and some others.

Architecture was there in the person of " Charles Barry in cool retirement at the top of the refreshment stairs, chatting with friends who passed that way. Mr. Alfred Waterhouse sheltered behind a large case of gigantic cups. The venerable Donaldson was seated under the wing of the Lord Mayor. Wyatt Papworth, leaning against a Corinthian pillar, took notes of the beauties present, invidious, perhaps, though not a laborious task ".

Edward, as best he could, moved about amid the dense and perspiring throng. Mercifully thin, he was able to jest with " G. A. Sala, whose countenance illuminated the gold and silver in the cases by which his image was reflected."[1]

Although the city presented a façade of affluence, in general the times were hard. Some of his projects at Turnham Green had not yet been started. The Fine Arts Society Gallery job, an improved entrance, was completed. It was only a minor undertaking, which assumed more importance on account of its situation. Architects were having a very thin time. To make things worse, Edward was taken ill and his doctor ordered him to stay at home, give up all nights at the theatre, abandon his morning and evening walks, thus breaking a lifetime's habit. A week of this regimen proved beneficial and he recovered sufficiently to be able to go and see Whistler's etchings, through his own doorway, at the Fine Arts Society Gallery in New Bond Street. They were the work he had done in Venice.

Inside, twelve impressions were pinned up on a maroon-coloured ground. The etchings were not arranged in sequence, and were only to be identified by chalk numbers roughly drawn by Whistler on the maroon cloth background. He found the show disappointing, one of Whistler's irritating gestures, specially stupid since this was his first effort to rehabilitate his fortune. He considered the etchings inferior to the Chelsea series, the best of those shown being, he thought, *The Doorway*. He did not hesitate to let Whistler know his opinion, that more care should have been taken to hang the etchings, a courtesy that would have cost nothing.

In the spring Godwin visited the Paris Salon and was even more disappointed by what he saw there than he had been by Whistler's etchings. Nothing but " suicides, dead Christs and the Inquisition make up the horror ". The only improvement he could note was that the pictures were more harmoniously framed than they had been in previous years. The " most fantastic fashion" had been adopted. He hastened, disconcerted, back to London.

When he got back to Westminster he found a letter from Ellen asking him to design her dresses and advise Irving on the presentation of *The Cup* by Tennyson. It was a generous gesture after all she had gone through for him. She was now firmly enthroned, having escaped from the anxiety of uncertain engagements through the union of her genius with that of Henry Irving. She had not forgotten Edward, for she had laid out Irving's garden in the same pattern as she had used long ago for her own at Harpenden. The cup, also, was to be designed by Edward. When it was completed it proved to be a three-handled cup standing upon three legs. As for Ellen's costumes, the most important dress was a toga in yellow, spangled with jewels. The original material, discovered by Ellen, had been woven by hand and the cost was twelve guineas a yard! They could afford only a specimen, and as the design needed the use of many yards, the problem was what to do next.

"You leave it to me," declared Arnott, the resourceful Yorkshire stage carpenter.

Left to himself, he bought some new silk, dyed it the same shade of saffron, and made two wood blocks, one for black, the other for red. Then he stamped the design on the orange ground, and when the material had been draped and some cheap spangles sewn on to it, the effect as seen by the audience was sumptuous. Naturally Godwin attended the performances. From his seat in the stalls he wrote a letter to Ellen, illustrated by sketches, suggesting modifications in some of her postures. The play ran for a hundred and twenty-five nights and then had to be withdrawn. On the hundredth night the cup which Edward had designed was given to Tennyson.

The unexpected success of this play was felt by the aesthetic to be an indication that their educative endeavours had at last borne some fruit. Whether it was due to the intelligence of the audience proving to be of a higher order than had been credited, the popularity of the principals, the excellence of the play or the name of the author, was debated and remained undecided. It could not be doubted that the public approval demonstrated that they were ready to see something different.

Of course Godwin felt encouraged. His confidence in the power of colour, sound and rhythm, co-ordinated as an artistic whole, had been endorsed by the public.

Nowadays he was "constantly receiving letters from architectural students asking for guidance as to the method to be pursued in their private studies". One wrote: "Knowing you to be a students' friend I should be greatly obliged if you would allow me to trouble you with a few lines."

In response Godwin wrote a set of papers for *The British Architect*. They are, as usual with him, the fruit of his own experience. He prefaced his remarks: "It is impossible to find in these or any other pages anything commensurate with the value of that direct personal influence which a wise master exercises on willing disciples. Nevertheless we will venture to shape some kind of answers to the queries we have received."

He explained that with him the day started at six and ended at ten. The time was not all spent in work and study. Walking, rowing, fencing, billiards, gymnastics and the theatre each had a portion in his time-table. Two hours were given to walking.

His advice on reading was prefaced by a list of books he had found most useful or helpful. "Take first of all three works and never part from them; for though they are not specially devoted to architecture, I know none so likely to help that faculty which reveals itself in what we call design. Taken in chronological order, these books are the Bible, Chaucer, Shakespeare. Or if you are not satisfied with this, take another triplet, Homer, Dante, Spencer. You see that in each set you get the antique world, the mediaeval, and the Renaissance."

The sum of his views was: "An architect's or artist's education is not to be found in words about architecture and art so much as in buildings, sculpture and painting and in careful illustration of them."

The third paper was on drawing. Coming from so remarkable a draughtsman, some of it must be quoted for the information his words give about his methods.

" Careful drawing is an exercise the young architect cannot have too much of : therefore always keep about you a fair-sized pocket book. I always carry one of Henry Penny's Patent, measuring 6″ × 3¼″, No. L.137, working with a very fine metallic point, and drawing as delicately and as firmly as I can. One great advantage of this kind of book is that you cannot rub out, and thus you early learn to draw only when you have something to draw. The scribbles that some people call ' sketches ' represent a certain amount of pen or pencil work, but I implore you not to encourage this abuse of drawing. There are architects who think it no doubt very fine and fancy that work of this kind is so artistic—so like an artist. . . . Buy the very best drawing materials you can get. Being valuable, you will not be so likely to abuse them with wasteful rubbishy usage. The tendency to play the fool with paper and pencil is so great that we occasionally see it ill-disguised in published works—a well-known and outrageous example is the interior view of the Reverend Newman Hall's chapel. In your pocket book jot down first thoughts for designs, very small and fine ; only be sure that they are thoughts and not mere wanderings and meanderings. You will possibly ask what you are to draw apart from design. Everything that is beautiful or that fully answers its purposes. If you come across a dead bird draw every detail of its wing or head or leg as carefully as you would delineate every feature of a thirteenth-century door or seventeenth-century staircase. Life is all too brief for you as architects to do anything worth doing with mountain, river or lake ; but with robin, patient on the snow-covered window sill, with the leaf that darkens the window pane, with the empty shell you pick up on the beach, or the fish that floats so steadily in your aquarium, you can do much. A design for a piece of carving from your hand would be worth

much could you draw a cock like Dürer. But above all things
be careful that the short-hand known as outline drawing be
not exclusively practised. You will never learn to grasp
form if you only draw outline. Much good architecture or
building depends almost wholly on its masses and disposition
of light and shade : its details, mouldings, carvings and so
on—give it a texture as it were and a special interest to near
views of bits and pieces of work; but the foremost beauty
and charm of building as building are always to be found in the
measure, the balance, the allotment of its lights and shades."[1]

In February, Whistler exhibited his Venice pastels. He had
worked hard during his stay there, to restore his fortunes.
The outcome was the fifty-three drawings hanging on the walls.
Most of the art critics were severe in their judgement, saying they
were unfinished. Godwin disagreed emphatically with them.
" These things are good," he asserted. " No. 4, *The Latterne*,
is a lovely composition with a high horizon; the brown paper,
with a touch, represents in value the quay from the base of the
drawing." When the artist read this he made one of his ironic
sallies: " They are not as good as I supposed, they are selling! "
Instead of flinging his pastels at the people as he had done
his etchings in his last show, Whistler had taken every precaution to make the exhibition a work of art. He had been scolded
by Godwin for his idleness over the etching display. Now every
detail had been thought out by them with care. The arrangement
of the pictures, the colour scheme of the room in Bond Street,
the mounts, the frames, all had been contrived to sustain the
effect. A low skirting of yellow gold, dull yellow green dado
cloth, then greengold mould, frieze and ceiling pale reddish
brown : frames and mounts rich yellow gold, some greengold.
The attendants were similarly dressed.
The critics were undecided about the decorative scheme.
What they wanted from the pictures can be deduced when we
read what Godwin had to say about his friend's latest work :
" As to the few bits of architecture he has drawn, he has given
us—with what remains of the marble forms and details, which

a knowledge of architecture would have tempted the eye to complete and restore and spoil—that most difficult of effects to render, its gradual decay. Of Venice as it is, in the dethroned, neglected, sad passing away of it, Whistler tells us with the hand of a master, who has sympathised with the noble city's sufferings and loss." This was not what the critics wanted. " The Ducal Palace, St. Mark's, The Bridge of the Rialto, the Fondaco di Tucht, San Georgio, or Sta Maria Della Salute, no matter whether vilely restored or not—all the familiar airs they wanted played again. They have sketches or photographs of them. They and their friends have played them so often that they fancy they know them and in some cases offends them even to the point of direct misrepresentation . . ." To etch the Venus de Milo, to paint the masterpieces of Phidias, to make pictures of the splendours of architectural genius, would be, to use his own words, " an impertinence. Things that are in themselves mighty and complete works of art should not do service to the other arts."[1]

As Mr. James Laver has said, Godwin " was almost his only champion ". For as yet Oscar Wilde was merely an ardent youthful admirer with " an extravagant, enthusiastic way of talking sense and nonsense that was most fascinating ".[2]

It is doubtful whether, if Wilde had not dramatised in his person the aesthetic movement, it would have been realised as existing, save by art historians. A kindred movement had been in being for some years before his arrival in London, due to the activity of William Morris and his circle, but the effect upon the middle classes had been disappointing. They had bought the more florid of his wallpapers and fabrics and in architecture they had broken up the normal formal civic elevation of the row of houses facing the street and had substituted for them a series of unrelated buildings. Godwin's own group in Tite Street, though designed by a single mind, revealed the disruptive effect of personal preferences even when for individuals of like mind.

The disappointment of Morris provoked him to change the character of his assault, and he changed also the section of society to which he addressed himself. From now on it was to be the

[1] *The British Architect*, February 25th, 1881, pp. 98–9.
[2] Louise Jopling, *Twenty Years of My Life*, p. 78.

workman and the working classes who were to bring about the reformation. Socialism was to supersede the comfortable individualism that had corrupted the middle classes.

The creative aesthetes favoured a different approach; they sought their support from among the artistically susceptible members of the leisured classes. Theirs, the aristocratic attitude, relied upon the imitative English to follow their lead. They even practised in life the gospel of Pater, " Not the fruit of experience, but experience itself, is the end."

They were encouraged by the contemplative aesthetes, those individuals who enjoy " without creating anything more permanent than conversation ", who were thrilled at the sight of a beautiful vase, enchanted by musical sounds, intoxicated by odours, sensitive to touch—all very foolish and reprehensible experiences in the opinion of their phlegmatic neighbours.

Alternative means of improving the taste of the average man or woman were suggested by Mary Haweis and others. They placed their confidence in art school training, designs by members of the Royal Academy, and the free admission of the people to museums and art galleries any day, but more particularly upon Sundays. John Ruskin supported her views with the difference that he thought that " a groat " should be charged for admission to any museum. All these proposals were adopted without any change in taste materialising.

The essence of the aesthetic doctrine was its exclusiveness. Only the elect could be moved by its nuances, only individuals so moved were capable of choice. " This recognition of the primary importance of the sensuous element in art, this love of art for art's sake, is the point in which we of the younger school have made a departure from the teaching of Mr. Ruskin—a departure definite and different and decisive."[1]

⊦. The aesthetes were the first to enjoy the healthy exercise provided by the invention of the bicycle, to play tennis in a discreet manner. Others among them may have yawned and described such strenuous conduct as vulgar, but even they benefited in body through merely reclining in a cushioned punt propelled by a young lady.

[1]Oscar Wilde, *Introduction to Rose Leaf and Apple Leaf by Rennell Rodd*, 1882.

What they did in the way of improving their furniture has been amusingly told by Sir Max Beerbohm in his essay, *1880*, when " they hurled their mahogany into the streets ". They favoured a less cumbersome style than their parents. As to the background, the wall became less aggressive and the pictures dispensed with their fruitful gilded frames. All this in houses pleasantly set in semi-rural Bedford Park, with communal facilities, club, school, church and pub. The aesthetes substituted simplicity for multiplicity, going part of the way toward a realisation that design is decoration, whereas Morris had thought that design and decoration were separate.

The activities of these enthusiasts were too much for the prosaic Aston Webb, who declared : " We have now certain well-known aesthetic villages not far from town, where people live in ' cots ' and fill their gardens with sunflowers, where ladies dress to suit the houses. . . . "

But it was Wilde who drew attention to the movement. Before his arrival there was little realisation by the million that anything unusual was afoot. The most explicit premonitory warnings were such as could be read into the few scattered drawings in *Punch* of children in Kate Greenaway costumes. Oxford, having housed Wilde for a space, knew more of what might be than London. Godwin had printed a sonnet of Oscar Wilde's written from Rome in 1879, although he was hardly an aesthete by adoption then. What had attracted wide notice to him on his arrival in town was the dress in which he is said to have walked in the West End. He was the movement's advertising agent, as little concerned with the product he pushed as the business man of that calling.

It soon became evident that he was not alone : by 1880 the appearance of Postelthwaite, Pilcox, Maudle, Mrs. Cimabue Brown in *Punch*, week after week, enabled the initiated to enlighten the less well informed by giving the puppets their real names of Wilde, Whistler, and Swinburne. *The World* and other newspapers joined in the sport and illustrated, reported or parodied the paradoxes of Wilde and his companions.

In April 1881 W. S. Gilbert and Arthur Sullivan added their opera *Patience* to the hubbub. It was designed to show the crowd, in a witty and friendly manner, what the aesthetic movement was. The introduction to the public of Wilde as *Archibald Grosvenor*,

> " *A pallid and thin young man,*
> *A haggard and lank young man,*
> *A Greenery-yallery, Grosvenor Gallery,*
> *Foot-in-the-grave young man,*"

and Swinburne as the poetic *Bunthorne*,

> " *A most intense young man,*
> *A soulful-eyed young man,*
> *An ultra-poetical, super-aesthetical,*
> *Out of the way young man,*"

made it impossible for anyone afterwards to ignore the cult and, least of all, to forget Wilde.

That clever young man took advantage of the occasion to publish his poems. Notoriety is of little satisfaction unless one has something to dispose of—and Wilde sold five editions! Other less able writers tried to reap some material benefit from the public interest in this latest artistic phase. A play, called *The Colonel*, by F. C. Burnand, the editor of *Punch*, followed *Patience*. Burnand had the knack and habit of writing farcical versions of serious works. This time his play was a renamed adaption of an old play, supposed to depict the discomfort attributable to living up to one's china. In it Wilde was represented thinly disguised as Lambert Stryke, the part being played by Beerbohm Tree. The character of Stryke was really unlike Wilde ; indeed it was a libel. The ubiquitous Howell appears more nearly like the part.

Still, *The Colonel* could not be missed by anyone so interested in the arts as Godwin, friend of one of the victims and acquainted with the others. Naturally he went to the Prince of Wales Theatre prepared to be entertained. *Patience* he had found charming. It is not unpleasant to witness the amusing travesty of our ideas or those of our friends ; points less initiated spectators may miss are appreciated and the play is all the more attractive. All things taken into account, he was disappointed by *The Colonel.* As was all too often his reaction, it was the setting, not the dialogue, that let down the play. One of the scenes was an aesthetic room. His own conception of such a room, and how it should be furnished, had been illustrated a month earlier.

The stage room, "presented to us as wrong, we find is furnished with artistic and simple things; a charming cabinet in walnut designed by Mr. Padgett for the green room, some simple inexpensive Sussex chairs like those sold by Messrs. W. Morris & Co., black coffee table after the well-known example originally designed in 1867 by the writer of these notes; a quite simple writing table, matting on the floor, a green and yellow paper on the walls, a sunflower frieze, a Japanese treatment of the ceiling (storks) and a red sun such as we see in Japanese books, and a hand screen, make up a scene which, if found wanting in certain details and forced in sunflowers, is certainly an intriguing room with individuality about it, quiet in tone, and, what is most important, harmonious and pleasing ".[1]

He came away persuaded that there was a conflict within the play and that the deductions to be drawn from it were not those intended by the author. Perhaps he treated the author too seriously.

Outside the theatre he met the leading lady. She passed unnoticed by the people in the street, although " her private costume, evidently new, was modelled line for line on that she had just worn as an aesthete in the comedy, and which the audience had been invited to ridicule ".

The play did no harm. Wilde was still looked upon as a contemporary poet who might in time develop into someone of consequence. Sunflowers, it is true, were greatly esteemed, but that they could provide a restrained decorative motive can be realised by those who have seen the wallpaper so named, designed by Bruce Talbot a few years earlier (1878) when it was awarded a gold medal at the Paris Exhibition at which Whistler and Godwin had shown their design for a room.

The year 1881 was a more prosperous year for everybody

[1] *The British Architect,* 1881, p. 379.

than had been the previous year. With it the demand for
Godwin's services as architect and stage designer increased. In
addition Whistler was discussing with him his project to build
another and yet more astonishing house. Thanks to Howell,
who was pushing the sale of his etchings, Whistler had recovered
from the shock of his lawsuit, and had taken up watercolour, the
earliest examples of which he had exhibited. One of them is in
Boston, America, a view of the Swan Pier and London Bridge.
It carried Edward's endorsement: "This is his first water-
colour." It was painted by the artist from Godwin's window
overlooking the Thames.

At this time, Edward and Beatrice Godwin were Whistler's
closest friends. The three were constantly together, whilst
sometimes it was Godwin and Whistler or Whistler and Mrs.
Godwin. The artist had become a great admirer of Beatrice.
He had made several drawings of her, one of the better being
named *Lamplight*. With her husband she attended the ex-
hibitions and *conversazione* of the St. Stephen's Art Club of which
they were founder members and regular exhibitors. At the club
they met Oscar Wilde, who talked at large to those who cared to
listen to him; pretty Mrs. Godwin, attentive, on one of the
settees.

It was borne upon Edward that time was slipping away.
One by one the men who had held leading places in the
architectural firmament had died. Upon him fell the mournful
duty of writing brief tributes to their memory. The first to go
was Sir Gilbert Scott. Only a few days before his death Edward
had travelled with him in a train going north. During the
journey Scott had spent the time in complaining of the lack of
appreciation of his work by his professional colleagues, and
Godwin had tried to comfort him. It must have seemed queer
to him that so successful a man should be in need of sympathy.
The next to pass was Burges, who, although slightly older than
Edward, died unexpectedly and prematurely as the result of a
cold caught in a train when returning from Bute Castle, Cardiff.
Never again was Edward to take tea with him in the garden
of Melbury Road, seated on a cold marble bench. Edward
had not seen much of Burges for some months, but for his earliest

and most constant friend he had nothing but affection, recalling
the days of their youth and their happy excursions in Ireland,
Shakespeare readings in Bristol and the days helping each other
at Blackheath or Harpenden. Then in December G. E. Street
died. The unhappy controversy over the Law Courts and the
large demands the superintendence entailed, the vacillation of
the Government, had proved too great a strain. Street had become
irritable and uncertain before his end. Edward wrote sympatheti-
cally about Street.

There was a queer symbolic mournfulness in the removal
one by one of these old warriors of the Goths in the Battle
of the Styles. Their climb had reached the summit; only
William Burges appeared to be on the way to the scaling
of higher peaks that Bodley, Seddon, Brooks and Butterfield
were in some measure to conquer. The three lost leaders had
accomplished something in that they had released architecture
from the bondage of ancient rules.

At the end of the year the trio, Whistler, Godwin and Wilde,
was broken up. Wilde had embarked on Christmas Eve and was
now in mid-Atlantic bearing to America the torch of the movement he had adopted as his own. Not unnaturally he felt proud
that he should have been chosen for this missionary enterprise.

The idea was that of the producers of the opera *Patience*
in America—they thought that the sight of a real live aesthete
would ensure the success of their enterprise. Wilde, hard
pressed for money, wanted to market a play that he had in his
pocket, *Vera*, and, having nothing better to do, accepted the
engagement.

Chapter XI

CHIEFLY CLOTHES

THE TWO elder men were relieved when Wilde had gone. His adulation had been occasionally embarrassing. News of his progress, and of how he had been entertained by millionaires, and how he had entertained his hosts, had been related from time to time in the London newspapers, and the gossip writer, George Augustus Sala, found his adventures a useful stop-gap.

Godwin had resigned his Fellowship almost as soon as he had been elected to the Council of the Institute, apparently because of some difference of opinion about the functions of that body. He had concluded that the regulation of architects and the relation of the profession to the people it served were insufficiently insisted upon by the governing council. Long ago he had made a number of suggestions upon the conduct of competitions and assessors, or as they were then called, " professional referees ". He proposed that competition drawings should be drawn in ink without any shading, that no perspective should be permitted and/or asked for ; for the promoters, that they should be obliged (1) to publish the award, (2) to abide by the award, and that the award of the assessor should be uninfluenced by the promoters' preferences. His experience, in particular from the disregard of the assessors' award, had been distressing. Now, seven years after he had made these reasonable suggestions (since adopted), nothing had been done and, naturally, he was averse from entering into any further unsatisfactorily regulated contests. Those architects outside the doors of the Royal Institute instanced his name as one of the several most able architects who declined membership, implying thereby that the Institute was unrepresentative and in need of internal reform. His name was frequently mentioned by speakers at meetings in Conduit Street, but too frequently in the past tense.

All the same he was still engaged in the design of numerous buildings; these, if they had been his sole occupation, would call for more attention than they will get here. As the work of any architect, they would not be negligible. Only because none of the buildings were of national consequence could it be thought that he was losing interest in architecture. Size is of no account—it is quality, not quantity, that has value. The querulous thought he should spend his life in designing town halls.

Among the buildings that may be mentioned are a house on the estate of Earl Ferrers, cottages at Moorgreen for Earl Cowper, and a parsonage at Moorgreen. (Earl Cowper and Godwin were united in an endeavour to save St. Alban's Cathedral from the restoring hands of Sir Edmund Beckett.) Another house was near Northampton, for Mr. Shuttleworth, a tea merchant, at Duston on the Harleston Road. It was built in the local stone manner with a straight drive from the road to the porch. " Shuttleworth wanted a bow window, but Godwin made various excuses, including the difficulty of curved window-panes. Shuttleworth said, 'Mr. Godwin, cannot you inscribe a polygon within a circle,' to which Godwin had to reply, 'Yes.' 'Well, Mr. Godwin, do it.' And Shuttleworth had his bow windows." The building is now known as Elmsleigh, and, though empty, is as left by Godwin. It was, for him, a reversion to a manner long discarded. In addition, he was employed on extensive works of varied types of building at Turnham Green, and several buildings for the church at Gaddesden. The houses at Turnham Green or Bedford Park, some of which were the first houses built in the estate, were the most interesting. They are more simple than their talked-about successors by Norman Shaw. They show unmistakably how acute was his sense of form; how appropriate his use of the southern vernacular. But while his competitors might weep their crocodile tears, and pretend that he was deserting the profession, others younger knew that his interest was as active as ever. They knew that his conception of the function of an architect was wider than other men's. They knew that he believed that such should be capable of revealing their genius, as had the great figures of the Renaissance, in all the arts and in all their actions. Only these were artists.

He still continued to conduct the design club of the *British Architect* as a public trial ground for young architects. The mere drafting of the periodical programmes occupied a great part of his time. The placing of the designs submitted made less diffi-culty than the drafting of the reports pointing out the reasons for his decisions, or the errors of the unsuccessful students, or the merit of the prize winner. His only reward was the regard of the young men of his profession, in whom he took more interest than any other practising architect. That they acknowledged.

Ever since he had first met Burges, Godwin had been hopeful that they might some time design a theatre. He was as well equipped as any man to undertake such a task, and possessed a greater knowledge of stagecraft, his colour sense and decorative genius being outstanding. Yet, despite his obvious aptitude, he had been overlooked. That winter there had been several fires in theatres, which had caused loss of life ; the public were disturbed by their frequency. Explaining that he had " closely studied this class of building for twenty years ", Godwin wrote a long report to Lt.-Col. Sir James McGarel-Hogg. It was divided into four sections : (1) the planning of the building, (2) the materials used in its constructions, (3) the mode of lighting, and (4) the management of the house.

About the materials (2) he wrote : " The materials used in the construction of theatres are, I think, more to be condemned than the inefficient planning. The outside or boundary of the parallelogram, and the walls of rooms that are rarely occupied, are built of brick and that not very soundly; then the circle in the heart of the parallelogram, with its two, three or four galleries— the place into which the audience is packed—is nearly always of *carton-pierre* and wood of slight scantlings, strengthened and supported by iron. Hardly anything more dangerous could be devised. There is in some houses a proscenium wall of brick, but the frame of the proscenium opening and the curtains, with their gearing, are of light, inflammable material. The stage, with its supports below, its painted scenery, its sur-roundings at the side (called ' wings '), its flapping ' sky boarders' above called 'flys', its gas battens, and the many movables too numerous for me to catalogue, it is no exaggeration to say, are a storehouse of fuel.

"The dressing-rooms are, in certain theatres, no better, and in some nothing more than ordinary dwelling rooms of low-class tenements, adapted to meet their present purpose, but without any special regard being shown for possible accidents by fire. Wood partitions, stairs and floors rendered very dry by the amount of heat caused by the gas consumed behind the scenes, are found in all sorts of places about the stage, sometimes under it, sometimes at the side, and sometimes at the back."

Under (3): the lighting of a theatre should be by numerous electric lights.

As to (4): "The servants in the front of the house are not only too few, but miserably inefficient, and the acting manager, so called because he is supposed to look after the audience and not the acting, is not always to be found when wanted. . . .

"The management of a theatre should be conducted on a system not merely courteous, but attentive."[1]

In the main the recommendations he made in 1882 were similar to those he had advanced in 1876.

The upshot of his report was a series of questions in Parliament about safety against fire. The subject was topical, not only when loss of life had occurred through fire, but, whenever an old theatre was reconditioned, or a new one built, Toole's *Folly Theatre*, King William Street, was in the first category, *The New Comedy*, Haymarket, and *The Savoy* in the last.

The owner of the latter, Richard D'Oyley Carte, was exceedingly proud of his building. Electric lighting had been installed, as recommended by Godwin, although actors long accustomed to gas did not like the effect upon their make-up as seen from the front, and were almost unanimous in considering the soft effect of gaslight to be preferable. *The Savoy* made some further change in decoration, the character of which change was made clear in a speech by D'Oyley Carte when *Patience* was moved from *The Opera Comique* to the *New Savoy* on October 10th, 1881.

[1] *The Building News*, January 27th, 1882, p. 106.

G

" Without adopting either of the styles known as Queen Anne and Early English or entering upon the so-called ' aesthetic ' manner, a result has been produced which I feel sure will be appreciated by persons of taste. . . . The main colour tones are white, pale yellow and gold."[1]

Simplicity had superseded multiplicity as a means of appeal. The cherubs, the angels, the trumpets had gone, and the aesthetes had prevailed in the colour scheme and drop curtain.

The White House was again in the news. When Whistler had been obliged to quit his Tite Street home he had left behind a portrait of his patron, F. R. Leyland, one of the committee of his creditors, whom he unjustly blamed for his financial difficulties. The picture was intended as a satire. It bore the crude title, *The Gold Scab*, and represented Leyland at the piano, on a music stool which "is an extremely uncomfortable one for men, whatever it may be for devils, for it is formed after the model of the White House ".[2] It was now sold by auction.

The same month the Grosvenor Gallery staged a one-man show of the life work of G. F. Watts, and, by coincidence, Ellen Terry's portrait by Louise Jopling. Watts had moved to Melbury Road and was now watched over by his neighbours, the Barringtons, who had helped him to persuade the owners of his pictures to loan them for the occasion. Watts was nervous lest the display should provoke adverse criticism and went to Brighton to escape from the fuss. He hardly need have done so, for the newspapers were kind and Watts decided it was less trying to be ignored than to be overpraised. Edward reviewed the collection of Watts' work, picture by picture.

In 1882 the reforming zeal of the aesthetes was extended to the subject of men's dress. It may surprise that the principal advocate of less formal wear for men was not Oscar Wilde, but an architect, not Godwin, but J. Alfred Gotch (who in 1923 became the President of the Royal Institute of British Architects). At the moment Godwin's interest in dress was mainly historical. He had just pulled up G.A.S. over the colour of a Franciscan's habit and that journalist had endorsed his letter—" Impudent cad ".

[1] Walter Hamilton, *The Aesthetic Movement*, 1882, p. 38.
[2] *The British Architect*, January 6th, 1882, p. 2.

This feud did not prevent his being elected the Honorary Secretary of the Costume Society which openly stated that they "had no scheme of dress reform". He at once commenced to prepare a series of plates to fill a portfolio consisting of forty drawings of historic costume each year. At long last he was to become his own Planché. He had followed the same path as a designer of costume as in his architectural development. He had adapted historic costume for the dressing of period plays. There was nothing original in that, nor in the demand for accuracy. His contribution was the attention he paid to colour as aiding the overall impression of the play's meaning.

In both arts—architecture and costume—his private preferences were prophetically in advance of the time. Dress worn by him at home, furniture designed by him for use, and decoration looked upon by others as queer were, in the course of years to be accepted as normal. Despite—nay, because of—his historic knowledge he recognised that clothing followed from the environment, material available, and energies of the wearer, and that similar conditions governed the evolution of furniture and the utilitarian arts. Hence the interiors of Portland Square and Taviton Street, and Ellen's and her children's clothes, and now Beatrice Godwin's gowns.

The same year as the Costume Society had been inspired to appoint him secretary (for he had not sought the situation nor taken any public part in the wide discussion about dress) some more interest had been awakened by a lecture of Mr. Frederick Treves on the unhygienic design of clothing worn by women. His talk was followed by an exhibition of hygienic clothing where specimens designed in Germany and America formed the chief exhibits. Mrs. Bishop's Rocky Mountain Travelling Costume provided a subject for the humorists. Although the divided skirt was shown among the exhibits it passed unnoted by the people who visited the exhibition. Before the Grundys could be awakened to the reality, it needed Lady Haberton to wear the garment and invoke protests of indecency. Someone inside the outfit is obviously needed to incite the attention of the English. Wilde had discovered their peculiarity.

Rather absurdly the agitation for a more rational dress for

women became mixed up in the public mind with the Women's Suffrage Movement. Properly the ideas upon the subject of dress reform came from the aesthetes, the younger members of the medical profession, and a provincial architect. They were forced to these proposals by the growing participation of women in industry, the improvement in public transport, the better construction of roads and changes afoot in the world.

Godwin knew full well that health was necessary for beauty to bloom; that for health pleasant surroundings and exercise were contributory factors; that suitable clothing would allow the wearer to breathe freely and to move gracefully. For years he had been advancing these ideas—to find for his pains that he was regarded, even among his friends, as a crank. It was mysterious and unfortunate that he should be unwell at intervals.

Ellen, his major experiment, had been allowed no corsets, hats or cosmetics, but instead kimonos and fresh air, to which rules she kept. In her autobiography she tells how for a lady who, she knew, doubted the nature of her marvellous complexion, she took the opportunity when at a party, to propose " follow my neighbour " as an entertainment and setting the example, vigorously washed her face. That put an end to doubt.

Oscar Wilde's American tour had been a financial success. With the money he had earned he was now in Paris, bestowing his poems on all the best people. Feigning that he was to emulate Balzac, he had resolved to change his style, and decided to become a cultivated Irishman. To complete the part, he had his hair trimmed and curled like a Roman. A fur-lined top coat of green cloth, with braid like a dressing-gown, was his remaining oddity.

When the money from America was spent he came to England and took rooms, three floors up, in a house in Charles Street, near Grosvenor Square. The rooms were furnished by his landlord, and there was little space for his few belongings. He was dangerously near the poverty line, but with his aplomb he put on a brave show. In this critical emergency someone suggested that the talks he had given in the States could be profitably repeated in this country. From Whistler, as a first step, he borrowed some notes for a talk he had been asked to give to the students of the Academy schools. In return he gave Whistler a complimentary advertisement. As yet, things were well between the two and Godwin. The more tedious provincial programme had yet to be commenced.

His first public lecture was on *America*, and was delivered in the newly built Princes' Hall, Piccadilly, the headquarters of the Institute of Painters. The audience was thin and bored. The lecturer appeared in " evening dress, tight-fitting trousers, white flower in button-hole, the shirt cuffs overlapping the sleeve as a schoolboy's collar overlaps his jacket, heavy seal hanging from a watch Albert of dark material ".[1]

It was noticeable how frequently the reporters of his lectures began with a description of his dress. The provinces still thought of him as strangely costumed. They were disappointed that his habit was not more freakish. Another added : " Mr. Wilde has a facile method of expression, and his attitudinising is not without a dash of picturesqueness. But he lacks purpose, pathos and power . . . he is better pleased with a negro melody than with the musical thunder of Niagara."[2] An observation that shows his, Wilde's, good sense.

The talks he gave in the provinces were on various themes, but the staple commodity was that on *The House Beautiful*. It was a compound of his conversation with Godwin and Whistler, the works of Ruskin and William Morris, decorated as yet by immature verbal ornamentation. Before and after the lecture he was entertained by some local notable sufficiently interested in the arts. He was advertised as the apostle of aestheticism, and as it was not generally known that he had altered his costume, his appearance—" a tall, well-built man, fully six feet in height, dressed in a suit of black broadcloth . . . a large white lily upon the left collar of his coat "—mildly surprised his audience. He spoke without notes.

" The kind of house most suited to England is the style commonly called Queen Anne, though it is a misnomer," were Stevenson's words in 1878. " The secret of all good architecture and all good furniture is to have the Greek line with the oriental phantasy." Wilde was still very hazy about architecture. He

[1] *The Illustrated London News*, July 14th, 1883, p. 27.
[2] *The Building News*, July 13th, 1883, p. 71.

probably thought, as did L. F. Day, that this was the source of Godwin's supremacy. On other subjects his observations were more penetrating: "Education is mistakenly founded on literature"; "Cultivate not memory but power of observation"; and, on family photographs: "Suppose you to make a stoical and Roman choice between relations and decorative art, I hope decorative art would be given first place."[1] "The wall is a background" and "the most beautiful room was a low room" was Edward.

Wilde's manner was very faintly and occasionally the Wilde of the future. "A fashion is merely a form of ugliness so intolerable that we are compelled to alter it every six months," was an early example.

On his return to London he rejoined his mentors. Whistler accepted Wilde's admiration—he had not yet realised that his thunder was stolen. With Godwin, Wilde was always on the best of terms. Still, like all popularisers, Wilde irritated the professors of the arts he advertised.

Wilde found that Godwin had been asked by the organisers of the Health Exhibition to write them a booklet on the subject of *Dress in Relation to Health and Climate.* While busy on this work, Godwin was constantly with Wilde, for the young man, in anticipation of his wedding, had taken a lease of 16 Tite Street, a plain, red-brick basement house with four floors over. A bay window to Tite Street passed through three floors.

Because it was desirable that his own surroundings should uphold his reputation, so widely noised, as a connoisseur of current taste, Oscar asked Edward to help him decorate the house in Tite Street. In consequence, the study on the uppermost floor was finished with white walls and woodwork and the furniture was painted red. Downstairs the walls were painted a buttercup yellow and the woodwork was lacquered in red. All the doors were removed and the openings were protected by curtains. Some, who had never seen the inside, said that the scheme was bizarre, and vaguely suggested it to be sinful. "Vulgarity is the conduct of others," stoically retorted Wilde.

The wedding at St. James's Church, Paddington, was an

[1] *The Architect,* December 1st, 1883, p. 337.

elegant affair. The church was full to see young Constance Lloyd married to Oscar. The bride, her six bridesmaids, and Lady Wilde wore costumes adapted from models ranging through the Medici to the aesthetic. After the honeymoon—Tite Street not being yet ready—the couple lived in his old rooms in Charles Street for some weeks.

In due course the Health Exhibition was set near the Albert Hall. The park was illuminated and the whole exhibition was on a grand scale, among the main attractions being a team of beautiful young women wearing gymnastic costume with coloured sashes, in which they demonstrated to music the benefit to be derived from eurythmics with dumb-bells. They were exquisite enough to persuade the most obstinate advocates of strait-lacing. It was fitting that Godwin, a pioneer of the movement toward sensible clothing, should have been asked to explain its theory. The subject was now one of the moment ; even architects were interested.

Of course, Wilde took the matter in hand. He had talked about this kind of theme in America where he had praised the cowboys for their sensible costume. He had worn a sensible outfit himself. Following Wilde's talk, the discussion was continued in *The Pall Mall Gazette*.

The interest that the controversy has for us lies in Wilde's references to Godwin. He called him to his aid in an attempt to rebut the opinion of Wentworth Huyshe that Greek dress was unsuited to the English climate. " One of the chief faults of modern dress is that it is composed of far too many articles of clothing, most of which are of the wrong substance ; but over a substratum of pure wool, such as is supplied by Dr. Jaeger under the modern German system, some modification of Greek costume is perfectly applicable to our climate, our country and our century. This important fact has already been pointed out by Mr. E. W. Godwin in his excellent, though too brief, handbook on Dress contributed to the Health Exhibition. I call it an important fact because it makes almost any form of lovely costume perfectly practicable in our cold climate. Mr. Godwin, it is true, points out that the English ladies of the thirteenth century abandoned after some time the flowing garments of the early Renaissance in favour of a tighter mode, such as Northern Europe seems to demand. This I quite admit, and its significance, but what I contend, and what I am sure Mr. Godwin would agree with me in, is that the principles, the laws of Greek dress, may be perfectly realised, even in a moderately tight gown with sleeves : I mean the principle of suspending all apparel from the shoulders and of relying for beauty of effect not on the stiff, ready-made ornaments of the modern milliner, bows where there should be no bows, and the flounces where there should be no flounces, but on the exquisite play of light and line that one gets from rich and rippling folds."[1]

This was the sort of conversation Edward Godwin had indulged in since the 'sixties. Later in the discussion Oscar referred to the booklet by Godwin again, this time as containing an illustration of the costume in which he had promenaded Piccadilly with a lily. The argument in *The Pall Mall Gazette* had become a dispute between the advocates of early seventeenth- and late eighteenth-century dress. Wilde favoured the earlier and Mr. Huyshe the later century. Oscar felt himself to be in a strong position because he had worn, and given up wearing, an eighteenth-century dress. " The subject," he wrote, " is in itself an interesting one ; I think it is worth continuing particularly as I have myself worn this late eighteenth-century dress many times, both in public and private, and so may claim to have a very positive right to speak on its comfort and suitabilities. The particular form of dress I wore was very similar to that given in Mr. Godwin's handbook, from a print of Northcote's, and had a certain elegance and grace about it which was very charming ; still, I gave it up for these reasons : After a further consideration of the laws of dress, I saw that a doublet is a far simpler and easier garment than a coat and waistcoat, and if buttoned from the shoulder far warmer also, and that tails have no place in costume, except in some Darwinian theory of heredity ; from absolute experience in the matter, I found that the excessive tightness of knee breeches is not really comfortable if one wears them constantly, and, in fact, I am satisfied myself that the dress is not one founded on any real principles."[2]

[1] Oscar Wilde, *Art and Decoration*, pp. 63–4.   [2] ibid., p. 68.

Unfortunately at this juncture, when he was writing on health, Godwin was himself far from well; he had even shown signs of impatience to the attitude of the philistines towards the opinions he so sincerely held. Though " the artist is not dependent on the visible and tangible ", he is in need of patrons. Twice recently he had declined to lecture to architects as such, and had only consented to speak to them as students of art. This was the aesthetes' creed, that the arts are one, on which he had spoken long before in Bristol. Now there were others emphasising the same notion : *The Century Guild* had been founded by Selwyn Image, Mackmurdo and Herbert Horne in order to co-ordinate the arts, and to provide in the journal of the Guild, *The Hobby Horse*, a means of spreading their views. Lord Leighton was actually trying to induce the Royal Academy to open its doors to the crafts and craftsmen.

About the critics, Edward went so far as to say : " There are not half a dozen individuals in any country who are capable of artistic discrimination." A few days later he supported his opinion in an article upon Whistler's portrait of Lady Archibald Campbell—*Le Brodequin Jaune*—a picture that few art critics appreciated. One of them had said : " Mr. Whistler has a capricious rendering of a lady dressed in black, in a black recess, on a dark green floor. She is turning affectedly half round towards the spectator as she buttons the *gant de suède* upon her left hand. . . . Its obvious affectation renders the work displeasing."

Beatrice Godwin had haunted Whistler's studio during the painting of Lady Campbell's portrait. The model was the latest of Edward's feminine admirers. Lady Archibald was a kindred spirit, passionately interested in artistic projects, a patron, and pardonably proud of the part she played. Her husband, a brother of the Duke of Argyle and a member of the Board of Coutts's Bank, shared her enthusiasm for the arts.

In July 1884, at the instance of Lady Campbell and her husband, *As You Like It* was performed in the open air. Naturally the whole of the arrangements were in the hands of Edward Godwin who, in addition to his usual roles, chose the actors and actresses for their several parts.

Herman Vezin as Jacques; Eleanor Calhoun, an American

actress, as Rosalind ; supported by Annie Schlitter in the role of
Celia ; George Foss as Adam, and others, the principal Orlando
being played by Lady Archibald Campbell herself. Godwin was
present in some of the scenes disguised as a friar. They called
themselves informally *The Pastoral Players* and disported their
persons in Coombe Wood adjoining the Campbell residence.
The play was a great success, and the performances were attended
by Royalty in the persons of the Prince and Princess of
Wales.

With his usual good nature Wilde wrote a eulogy of the
comedy. He insisted that it had gained in interest when set in
the surroundings of nature.

" At least it seemed so to me. The Duke and his companions
were dressed in serge tunics, leathern jerkins, high hoods and
gauntlets, and wore by-cocket hats and hoods. As they were
playing in a real forest they found, I am sure, their dresses
extremely convenient. To every character in the play was given
a perfectly appropriate attire and the brown and green of the
costumes harmonised exquisitely with the ferns through which
they wandered, the trees beneath which they lay and the lovely
English landscape that surrounded the Pastoral Players. The
perfect naturalness of the scene was due to the absolute accuracy
and appropriateness of everything that was worn." It only
remains to add that Lady Campbell looked bewitchingly lovely
in her costume as Orlando.

That Godwin's reputation and social attachments could be
used to advantage was realised by *Liberty's*. They enlisted his
services " for the study and execution of costumes, embracing
all periods of historic dress, together with such modifications of
really beautiful examples as may be adapted to the convention-
alities of modern life without rendering them eccentric or
bizarre.

" It is purposed to make a continued and systematic attempt
to establish an Educational School of Personal Adornment,
when shall be secured such forms, draperies, colours and ornaments as harmonise most perfectly with the natural characteristics
of the wearer ; and where shall be provided for amateurs, artists
and the stage the most beautiful types of modern dress, and the

most reliable reproductions of ancient costume, plain or rich, according to the requirements of the person or the character."[1]

The newspapers captioned the announcement with the words : " A Curious Experiment." Why anyone should be surprised is not apparent. The stage had for years employed the services of male costume designers, and that their skill and taste should be denied the laity would not seem reasonable. The private views which he arranged were unique and might have been expected to provoke some similar headline, because mannequins were employed and the dresses shown, " all worn by ladies whose stature and personal appearance was singularly in harmony with their style and dress ". It may have been the first occasion when such a parade was held in England, though in her autobiography Lady Duff Gordon claims to have been the earliest to have used living models. She must have been mistaken.

In retrospect *Liberty & Co.'s Catalogue, 1890,* recalled the epoch-making decision in the following words :

" ' *Liberty* ' *Developments in Form and Colour*
Recollections. There are many within the inner circle of art and fashion who remember in the spring of 1884 Messrs. Liberty's first experimental efforts as exponents of ' a new school of dressmaking ' : originated in opposition to certain meaningless and extravagant vagaries, and to frequent vulgarisms of mid-nineteenth-century ' Toilettes ' and Costumes.
The New Departure. The new departure was undertaken with no desire for ' change ' as a mere freak of fashion, but on principle and to secure veritable and beneficial results. The late gifted artist, architect and archaeologist, Mr. E. W. Godwin, in concert with the founder of the house of Liberty & Co., gave in advance much thought and consideration to the problem, though, as a matter of detail, neither of the initiators claimed or necessarily possessed any special knowledge of the technicalities connected with the mysteries of ' the professional modiste '.
The Object Aimed At. The immediate aim was to re-establish the craft of dressmaking upon some hygienic,

[1] *Liberty & Co.'s Catalogue, 1890.*

intelligible and progressive basis ; to initiate a renaissance that should commend itself artistically to leaders of art and fashion, and to challenge on its merits the heretofore all-powerful and autocratic fiat of Paris for ' change ' and ' novelty ' so far as it was oblivious of grace or fitness."

Edward was intensely interested in this aspect of the movement. If the women could be persuaded to adopt the costume designed to suit their personality, or reasonably accommodating to their occupation, not a difficult enterprise, their influence would extend its persuasive effect over ever-increasing numbers. Indeed it followed that women would demand a setting to match their refinement, thus the whole of the visual arts would be enlisted in their service, and the mechanical inventions adapted to minister to their demands. Of course it was not intended to imply that the furniture or decoration of a room should be altered as frequently as dress ; on the other hand it was felt that greater stability in costume design would follow.

A further opportunity to co-ordinate the arts was afforded to him when he was engaged by Wilson Barrett to dress and produce *Claudian*. The presentation provoked the customary dispute between the appreciators and depreciators. The critics said that there " should be more of the life and less of the death of Claudian ". Wilde was ranged with those who were pleased by the ensemble. In *The Truth of Masks* he paid this compliment :

" Indeed, there is not the slightest necessity that the public should know the authorities for the mounting of any piece. From such materials, for instance, as the disc of Theodosius, materials with which the majority of people are probably not very familiar Mr. E. W. Godwin, one of the most artistic spirits of this century in England, created the marvellous loveliness of the first act of *Claudian*, and showed us the life of Byzantium in the fourth century, not by a dreary lecture and set of grinning casts, not by a novel which requires a glossary to explain it, but by the visible presentation before us of all the glory of that great town."

Turning to the disappointed, Wilde replied, " Only the foolish called it pedantry, only those who would neither look nor listen spoke of the passion of the play being killed by its paint. It was in reality a scene not merely perfect in its picturesqueness, but absolutely dramatic also, getting rid of any necessity for tedious descriptions, and showing us, by the colour of and character of Claudian's dress and the dress of his attendants, the whole nature and life of the man, from what school of philosophy he affected, down to which horses he backed on the turf."

Whistler was asked by Edward to come and see the performance. He accepted the invitation and brought along with him his latest pupil, Mortimer Mempes. The three sat together, and Mempes and Godwin were astonished by the reaction of Whistler, who laughed and rocked " to and fro in an agony of merriment ". What he found amusing they could not understand. Mempes, who looked on Godwin as " a serious sort of fellow ", noticed that Edward found difficulty in not joining in their companion's inexplicable hilarity.[1]

Although Whistler might laugh, and some of the critics find fault, Wilson Barrett was gratified by the support of his public, they approved the play : he retained Godwin to assist him in staging *Hamlet*, the history he had chosen for the autumn season. In order to get the proper atmosphere, Edward went to Copenhagen, and thence to Elsinore.

Hamlet was put on at the Princes' in October, and ran to full houses well into the following year.

[1] Mortimer Mempes, *Whistler as I Knew Him*, p. 9.

CHAPTER XII

THE END OF THE JOURNEY

IN JANUARY 1885 Lady Archibald Campbell and her friends met and decided to form a group to perform plays in the open air. The meeting was the outcome of the Charity Performance the year before, which had been such a pleasurable social and artistic event that they were eager to extend the experience. In later years Lady Archibald claimed to have been the first person to have suggested this kind of entertainment. The party resolved to confirm the name of their society—*The Pastoral Players*—and planned to give nine performances during the year.

Edward was again appointed what the newspapers described as " The Director General of Entertainments ". Their earlier success had been of his making, and undoubtedly he was, in experience and ability, the only possible choice. He enjoyed the work, and knew and was known to all the difficult actors, amateur and professional; it was in fact he who selected them. In addition he had that air of authority with the men and charm with the ladies which, united to their admiration for his brilliance, ensured the smooth running of the entertainment when at last the exacting rehearsals had been approved.

Some of his friends among the architects regretted that he was giving so much of his time to theatrical business. At the Royal Institute, when a few of his drawings were shown as specimens of draughtsmanship, it was voiced of him: " That gifted architect of whom more yet was to be expected than he has given the world." His immediate response was a design for a town church to be erected in London, a building of bold, simplified Gothic; besides, he was already far advanced upon the design of a new house for Whistler. It was little use architects saying that they looked to him for a larger output when any patronage they could influence was not for him. If they had been serious in their praise they would have reformed the competition creed.

Edward did not complain, he had more than enough to interest him and keep him occupied. There were the plates for the Costume Society to be drawn; there was a long article on the remarkable house in Melbury Road and its contents to be written now that the death of Burges had drawn even more wide attention to it. Furthermore, some of his furniture made by William Watt was on exhibition. The pieces, though grounded upon a study of historic styles, Greek and Jacobean, were markedly superior to any contemporary furniture, and have an elegance that has not been surpassed by any designer. Though appreciated by some few connoisseurs and young people, they were too costly for all but rich, newly married couples. His sideboards and chairs needed to be lived up to in the 'eighties. Realising this drawback, he designed a number of pieces in a utilitarian manner then quite novel, but now quite modern.

Moreover, while he was not building any large town hall, he had a host of small jobs to attend to, apart from various theatrical undertakings. In fact, he was attempting too much. In February he was again unwell. These breakdowns were becoming alarmingly frequent and the doctor ordered him to bed. It was unfortunate, for he was unable to preside at a meeting of the Society for the Encouragement of the Fine Arts. In spite of what others called " his personal shortcomings " he had at last become recognised as a great artist. The occasion was a lecture by G. C. Haité, on wallpaper design. He was very disappointed, for he was so scrupulous in fulfilling his engagements, that any inability to do so troubled him. Yet the doctor was adamant, and so he obeyed.

The lecture was illustrated by a collection of drawings for wallpapers by Edward Godwin, Walter Crane, William Morris, Lewis F. Day, and some other artists. Actual pieces of paper printed from their designs, lent by Woolams & Co., Jeffrey & Co., Tolman, and Sanderson, were hung on the walls.

In Godwin's absence, the lecturer and the rest of the speakers in the discussion that followed referred to his outstanding contributions to the art of wallpaper over many years. A Frenchman present drew special attention to one of his first designs as epoch-making. It was perhaps as well that Edward was spared the embarrassment of so much praise.[1]

The rest in bed did him good and he was able to attend the talk by Whistler at the Princes' Hall on February 20th, 1885, a week later. Whistler announced his performance as *ten o'clock*, the hour when the proceedings were to begin. For weeks past he had rehearsed his effects on the Embankment under the stars, had discussed the subject matter in his studio and Godwin's chambers with Edward. His theme in the main consisted of the material he had jotted down for Wilde's talk to the Academy students, and now when he wanted to speak he came to regret bitterly that he had ever given his thoughts away to Oscar. Edward knew his theme by heart.

On the crucial night Wilde and Edward were interested auditors. The setting in the Princes' Hall had been arranged by the D'Oyley Cartes, who had planned Wilde's visit to America and were now making a fortune out of the Gilbert and Sullivan operas.

The lecturer stood before a plain, unadorned background, dapper in evening dress. Not being used to public speaking, his voice did not carry as well as it should in spite of his constant demosthenian-like practice near the Thames. In this respect he fell far short of Wilde at whose expense he strove hard to be amusing. The audience had expected to be entertained. *The Times* observed that the crowd came to hear him in the hope that the " eccentric genius of the artist would find them amusement for an hour ".[2] Those who could hear were not disappointed.

" The people had been harassed by art in every guise, versed with many methods as to its endurance. They had been told that they shall love art, and live with it. Their houses have been invaded, their walls covered with paper, their very dresses taken to task, until roused at last, bewildered and filled with doubts and discomforts of senseless suggestions they resent such

[1] *The Building News,* February 20th, 1885, p. 277.
[2] *The Times,* February 21st, 1885, p. 7.

intrusion and cast forth the false prophets who have brought the very name of the beautiful into disrepute, and derision upon themselves." Some of this was intended for Oscar. And of Ruskin : " Sage of the universities, learned in many matters and of much experience in all save his subject." And at the enthusiasts for Queen Anne : " And so, for the flock, little hamlets grow near Hammersmith and the steam horse is scorned." Aston Webb had already said much the same. The lecturer obviously enjoyed himself after his own fashion. While some of his quips were critical of Edward, he smiled with the rest. Wilde took the whole good-naturedly, differing from " The master " on some points, and on costume in particular. They both knew Whistler too well to be annoyed.

" I hardly think that pretty and delightful people will continue to wear a style of dress as ugly as it is useless and as meaningless as it is monstrous, even on the chance of such a master as Mr. Whistler spiritualising them into a symphony or refining them into a mist. For the arts are made for life, and not life for the arts," observed Wilde, less rudely.

Whistler was well satisfied with his performance ; so pleased that some years later he published his discourse as a part of his decoratively printed book, *The Gentle Art of Making Enemies*, a title that leaves no doubt as to his intention to exasperate, and so awaken the audience and stimulate their attention. He had always been a sharp-tongued conversationalist. " If I died before Jimmy, he would not have a friend left in a week," explained Beatrice Godwin in after days when she had become the artist's wife. Probably because of her influence over Whistler, he was able to associate amicably with Edward even when the architect turned the tables upon him and censured him for his work. The two painters had formed an unconcealed attachment for each other. Whistler escorted her everywhere when her husband was engaged in his profession or busy endeavouring to reconcile a galaxy of women amateurs and professional actors in their parts. Though they remained friendly, the Godwins had agreed to part the year before and were living, she in Oxfordshire and he in London.

The setting in which the Pastoral Players performed was

the grounds of Coombe House, Dr. M'Geach's hydropathic, a choice which gave some people opportunity for hilarity, since the costumed actors, during the weeks of rehearsal, could be mistaken by the unwary for the patients. The Prince of Wales headed the distinguished list of patrons of the first performance, and subsequently he and his Princess were often present.

Although the weather was unfavourable that year, and a few of the prearranged dates had to be changed, Society put up its umbrellas and persistently supported the Royal spectators. Of all the entertainments, *The Faithful Shepherdess*, by John Fletcher, was voted as particularly attractive. " Mr. Godwin's arrangement of his tableaux is thoroughly effective, and when we consider the immense difficulties that not only the manager but the actors and actresses have to contend with, we cannot speak too highly of the whole performance."[1] The beautiful Lady Archibald Campbell represented Peregot, and Amoret was played by Princess Hellen of Kappurthala. When it was over the Prince of Wales congratulated the producer, and the performers were presented to him.

In playing the part he did, Godwin was taking a place in the initiation of a revolution in theatrical presentation, in that through his specially endowed person he was asserting the importance of the producer in the presentation of the play, and this at a time when the actor-manager was the accepted arbiter, when plays were written for them and not as works of art. We know how he had become able to handle the reins of the team, costume, setting and words. We do not know how he gained his right to prescribe actions, for there is no record of his ever having played any part save that of a friar—and then only to be able to be unobtrusively present during the scene, yet he had had the temerity to tell a Terry how to move on the stage.

In the early months of the following year Godwin was almost solely immersed in the preparation of the play of Sophocles, *Helena in Troas*. The entire management was left in his hands, costumes, setting and the selection of the performers. It was to be the most perfect of the several entertainments that had shown London the beauty of Greek Art and costume. In the winter

1 *The Graphic*, July 4th, 1885, p. 3.

From *The Graphic*, June 5th, 1886.

HELENA IN TROAS.

some of the members of the Royal Academy had sponsored a ball to which the ladies were invited, dressed as Grecian damsels. It had not been an unmixed success. On this account the promoters of *Helena* were nervous lest the play would prove too intellectual to attract, so that probably the adventure would cost more than the receipts would cover. As a precaution they collected guarantee promises amounting to £1,000 against this contingency, and as an additional insurance they were permitted to announce that the Prince and Princess of Wales would honour the first performance by their attendance. The Prince was very generous of his time in favouring these innovations with his nominal support. Without this some of the projects would not otherwise have had enough appeal.

The play was from a translation by Todhunter. *Helena* was designed to be staged in Hengler's Circus in Great Pulteney Street. It was intended to be shown for a fortnight. The circus had only just been rebuilt from the ground up, and every part of the building was new and resplendent. Whether it was the form of the arena which suggested the conception, or, as is more probable, Godwin's knowledge of the Greek Theatre, that led to the selection of the ring, matters little. The novel feature of the staging was that the actors were in front of the dais and in close relationship with the spectators. If the reader wants to realise how very advanced in design the arrangement was, he has only to compare the illustration in *The Graphic* for June 5th, 1886 (which shows the setting for *Helena*), with that of the Theatre at Malmo, built sixty years after, shown in *The Architectural Review* in the month of March, 1946. The resemblance is sufficient to persuade the most sceptical.

" In the Greek play the chorus appeared in the orchestra, that is, in the midst of the audience, while the personages, masked and heightened, were seen in ghostly illusion of grandeur on the stage."

The play was in blank verse, a form which Oscar Wilde attributed " more to the courtesy of the printer than the genius of the poet ".

The people Edward had chosen to take the several parts were as follows : Miss Alma Murray represented Helena ; Hecuba was to be portrayed by Lucy Roche; Tree was Paris (he held a high opinion of Godwin's stage-craft); Mrs. Tree, Aenone; Herman Vezin, an intellectual actor, who had been a consistent patron of his, took the part of Priam. There were several more, some of whom joined ultimately the familiar names in their profession. The cast was completed by a crowd of ladies, prominent in their day as beauties. They were led by Constance Wilde, who took the part to please her husband, and Louise Jopling, the lively and handsome artist. These two were attendants upon Helena. " The stage curtains slowly divided and from the house of Priam came forth Helen herself, in a robe woven with all the wonders of war and broidered with the pageant of battle. With her were her two handmaidens—one in white and yellow and one in green."[1] So wrote Oscar in his enthusiastic description of the spectacle.

The last named of the maidens, Mrs. Jopling, was a beautiful brunette, whose portrait by Millais had been a sensation. She tells in her book of recollections, *Twenty Years of My Life*, how she came to be playing her small part. It appears that she wanted to paint a picture with a Grecian theme, and, learning that the play *Helena* was in rehearsal, she instantly decided that if she could witness the preparation she would be able to glean some inspiration and probably find a model. So she telegraphed to Edward, whom she knew slightly : " May I attend a rehearsal ? " Back came his reply : " Come and help."

Thus encouraged, she wasted no time, took a hansom and drove to Hengler's. Louise Jopling knew everybody and everyone knew her. She was lovely and likeable, a plucky woman who had overcome private troubles and social prejudices that would have daunted or broken most Victorian females. She had earned her place as a painter, and among her many friends were Oscar Wilde and his wife, Jimmy Whistler, William Burges, who had been the architect of her studio and had persuaded himself that, should she become a widow, he would make her his wife ; and Princess Louise, who as an artist, was frequently in her studio. She had painted a portrait of Ellen. All the company gathered to play *Helena* already knew her.

[1]Oscar Wilde, *Reviews*, p. 69.

As soon as Louise arrived, Godwin asked her to join the party. He suggested that she play, with Constance Wilde, the role of one of the attendants upon Helena. She would make, he said, a striking contrast with her brunette beauty to the pretty, fair-haired Constance. Hardly pausing to reflect, Louise Jopling accepted the invitation to help. That settled, Edward told her to arrange some of the women in the same attitude as those on the Parthenon frieze. The ladies who had to represent the sculpture were dressed in unbleached linen that gave them a striking likeness to pentelic marble.

Mrs. Jopling knew as much about Godwin as anyone. It was to her that Ellen had written when he had so suddenly married a second time. She thought him fascinating—and confessed that he was for her a reincarnation of an ancient Greek—when others found him indifferently like Cardinal Manning or Henry IV of France. For he was now clean-shaven and grey-haired.

At long last the opening evening came; the Prince and Princess attended, as they had promised, and were supported by the principal figures in all walks of life. One of them, Oscar Wilde, wrote a laudatory account of the performance in the *Dramatic Review* for May 22nd, 1886.

" One might have thought that to have produced *As You Like It* in an English forest would have satisfied the most ambitious spirit; but Mr. Godwin had not contented himself with his sylvan triumphs. From Shakespeare he has passed to Sophocles, and has given us the most perfect exhibition of a Greek dramatic performance that has as yet been seen in this country. . . .

" In the centre of this circle, which was paved with the semblance of tesselated marble, stood the altar of Dionysios, and beyond rose the long shallow stage faced with casts of the temple of Bassae, and bearing the huge portal of the house of Paris, and the gleaming battlements of Troy."[1]

The general press was, as it had frequently shown itself to be, cold yet civil.

[1] Oscar Wilde, *Reviews*, p. 69.

" Good society is very easily bored, yet it will endure
boredom with a truly Spartan patience if only some benevolent
fairy will whisper in its ear that the entertainment which it is
asked to patronise is fashionable.

" Mr. Godwin carried out his intention very successfully.
The arrangement of the stage and interior were as much as
possible in accordance with the rules of Greek art. The scene
was simple but majestic."

That was a fair instance of their comment. Mr. Todhunter's
verse may have been tedious.

Yet although the suggestion of the critics was that the production was above the heads of the spectators, that they were
there to be talked about, or to be able to claim that they had
witnessed the spectacle, *Helena in Troas* was a success. It ran to
full houses, without the added attraction of the Royal visitors,
and in spite of, or maybe because of, the punctuation of the
script. At the end of the last performance Godwin was called
before the curtain. Seddon, who was present, declared that
Edward had never appeared to such advantage and of so much
consequence as he did on that memorable evening. Not a penny
of the guarantee fund was needed. Instead there was a considerable profit, to use some of which two extra performances
were given at reduced prices, and to take the production on tour
with a slightly different set of actors.

All of those concerned were highly elated ; the financial success
of the Greek play went to their heads. So convinced were
they that they knew what the public wanted that Godwin and
some of his friends were tempted to try their fortune in the
dangerous realm of theatrical speculation. There was money
in it.

In particular two sisters, Miss Steer and Mrs. Mackintosh,
both young society belles ambitious to display their talent,
easily persuaded Godwin and some others to join them in
financing and producing a play. The party combined to rent
the *Opera Comique*, the little theatre at which *Patience* had first
been heard. Rather unexpectedly, the play they chose to revive
was an old work of Tom Taylor's, *The Fool's Revenge*, adapted

by him from the French, *Le Roi s'Amuse*. The cast was, as it had been in *Helena*, a combination of amateur and professional actors. Herman Vezin was the best known of the professionals, the Steer ladies the most prominent amateurs.

The play was put on in July. Everything that could be thought of had been done to attract the theatre-goer, new actresses and the curiosity they were expected to arouse, the circle of friends they would draw ; new costumes, new scenery, both as attractive as the taste of Godwin could devise. They rehearsed until they were word and action perfect. But the large audience failed to materialise. The failure could not be placed upon Edward's shoulders, unless he could be accused of lack of judgement of the time of year appropriate for the venture. It was the month of July ; that was too late in the year. The weather was unbearably hot and London wanted to be by the Thames, by the sea, or in the north. Worse still, the country was irritated and disturbed by the General Election forced upon the electorate by Mr. Gladstone's Home Rule proposals. The balance sheet showed that the adventure was a failure, and that Edward and his admirers had lost their money. They decided to give up the ill-advised speculation before they had lost all. The play was not of the character suited to Godwin's talents, nor to those of Herman Vezin.

Happily the conditions that had told against *The Fool's Revenge*, fine weather and heat, late season and the election out of the way, united to admit of the Pastoral Players rejoicing over a succession of successes, attracting crowds of spectators who compensated by their attendance for the misfortune of the year before when the weather had been hostile. This year the setting had been changed. " Lady Campbell and her faithful band of Pastoral Players are this year to bring their open-air performances nearer town. The lovely grounds of Dr. M'Geach's hydro at Coombe are forsaken for the pretty patch of glade and woodland pertaining to Mrs. Leo Schuster's villa by the Ridgeway at Wimbledon. No doubt Mr. Godwin has had an eye to the capabilities of the new locale as a background for the pastoral scene of Lord Tennyson's *Becket* ", which had been re-styled *Fair Rosamund*.

Once again the Prince and Princess of Wales, this time with the children, attended the show. The tickets, one guinea each, were sold out and the road to Wimbledon was dusty with carriages. In addition to the appeal to the eye and ear, the palate was titillated. " Delicious too were the plates of fresh strawberries with clotted cream."

Of the series of performances, *As You Like It* was voted the favourite. It had been their first success and was understood best by both players and spectators.

These two enterprises, *Helena in Troas* and the open-air plays, were the climax of Godwin's achievements as a producer. Because of their remarkable effectiveness he was acknowledged as " unsurpassed as a setter of plays ".

The vocal difficulties of the members of the Pastoral Players in the open air, some of them amateurs who needed tactful handling, had been overcome by his selection of the site, for its acoustic properties, the choice of part they should play, and the staunch support of Lady Archibald Campbell of him and his ideals. Into an atmosphere of acute individualism he had imported a communal spirit akin to the Elizabethan or earlier players. All this had been contrived at a time when he was periodically unwell and had often to rest under his doctor's orders. It was only because it had been his lifelong habit to do with all his might that which he had set himself to do that he was able to support the strain. Yet in the intervals between his pageant productions, he spent much time examining the designs submitted by students of the British Architects Design Club, writing his reports on their work and thinking out new problems to set for their solution. No one realised the pains he took, nor the effort he expended on their behalf.

His friend Whistler's intended new house had at last progressed to the final stage. The plans had been deposited with the authority. Like its forerunner, it had been the subject of much discussion between the client and his architect. Now, however, that was all ended, the artist was bubbling over with excitement about the project, to such a pitch that writing from Godwin's office in Westminster, on Edward's notepaper, to Louise Jopling, he grew lyrical over the drawings—" they are simply ravishing and you will immediately construct with Godwin something lovely for yourself ".

He had called at Edward's chambers, as was his habit, and had found him ill in bed, attended by Martha Collins. Though his health had been indifferent for the past two years, none of his associates thought his condition to be serious, nor did he himself feel that there was much amiss, for a few days' rest always saw him up and about again. It was troublesome not to be sure that he would be able to keep his promises. The letter that Whistler wrote evidences the optimism of his friends, for in it he was trying to induce Louise to make up her mind and act, the action desired of her being to build a " palace " next door to his own. Mrs. Jopling, like Whistler, was meditating building a new house. She had been offered a tempting sum for the remainder of the lease of her house, and the garden studio designed by Burges. It was situated on the site of the one-time home of Sir Thomas More. There was a tree in the garden under which he had sat. The Catholics wanted to buy the place. They planned to turn the studio into a chapel. She had already consulted Edward as to the advisability of accepting their offer. His reply was to the effect that she should accept the terms, and remove to some temporary address in Chelsea until a new house could be made ready for her occupation. His letter to her ended : " The next move I make is to St. Peter's Hospital, where I have bespoken a ward all to myself ; then the next ward may be $6 \times 4 \times 2$. I feel completely done with life." It was written at the end of August 1886. His gloomy foreboding was too true. Louise Jopling's dream house was never to exist other than in his mind. He was alone and in pain. At last it was realised by his friends that he was gravely ill. Beatrice Godwin was called home from Paris.[1]

Lady Archibald Campbell called and was kind in her attention, telling him of the success of the players at Coombe Wood. Whistler visited him every day. It was plain that he was very ill, dying.

In an attempt to save him, Mr. Adcock, assisted by two other surgeons, operated upon him. The attempt was of no avail and the patient never rallied from the anaesthetic. Still unconscious,

[1] Louise Jopling, *Twenty Years of My Life*, p. 291.]

just before midnight on the same day, October 6th, he died. With him at the end were his wife, Lady Archibald Campbell and James McNeill Whistler, his friends.

There was nothing they could do but wait for the morning. Before dawn, Whistler left the house in the dark to walk to his brother's to tell him the news. But for Dr. Whistler the information was no surprise; he already knew by some premonition, in fact he had told his wife, that Edward was dead— at the very moment that he had indeed died.

From Dr. Whistler's, when dawn broke, James hurried through the misty streets to awaken Louise Jopling, to ask her to go and tell Ellen what had happened. He wanted to spare her the shock of reading the tidings in the morning papers.

Mrs. Jopling dressed at once and went on her difficult mission. Never after could she still the memory of the cry that greeted her message: " There was no one like him! "

It was not generally known that Edward was dead until a week later when *The Times* of October 14th, 1886, bore an announcement of the death on the 6th at Great College Street, Westminster, of Edward William Godwin, F.S.A.

By then he had already been buried. The funeral had been curious. Mrs. Godwin, Lady Archibald Campbell and Whistler, had accompanied the coffin from London. Then it had been placed onto an open farm wagon. Into this the three mourners had clambered; when covering up the coffin they had used it as a table for the alfresco meal eaten as they jolted along in the autumn air through the country lanes, to the last resting place of a genius, " the corner of a field " at Northleigh, near Witney, in Oxfordshire.

Someone (it seems most probable that the poet was Oscar Wilde) wrote of him this sonnet:

> " *A man of men, born to be general king,*
> *By frank election of the artist kind,*
> *Attempting all things, and on anything*
> *Setting the signet of a master mind.*
> *What others dreamed amiss, he did aright,*
> *His dreams were visions of art's golden age,*

Yet self betrayed he fell in Fortune's spite,
His royal birthright sold for scanty wage.
The best of comrades, winning old and young
With keen audacious charm, dandling the fool
For blatant pedants of the bungler school.
They tell me he had faults, I know of one
Dying too soon, he left his best undone."

It was found among Dame Ellen Terry's papers.

INDEX